How To Set Up Your Home or Small Business Network

Other Titles of Interest from Bernard Babani (publishing) Ltd

BP514   Windows XP Explained

BP515   Getting the Most from Windows XP

BP521   Easy Windows XP Troubleshooting

BP538   Windows XP for Beginners

BP549   Easy PC Wi-Fi networking

BP550   Advanced Guide to Windows XP

BP557   How did I do That ... in Windows XP

BP563   Using Windows XP's Accessories

Other Titles by the same authors

BP565   Using Microsoft Windows XP Media Center 2005

How To Set Up Your Home or Small Business Network

by

Tony Campbell

&

Andrew Edney

Bernard Babani (publishing) Ltd

The Grampians

Shepherds Bush Road

London W6 7NF

England

www.babanibooks.com

Please Note

Although every care has been taken with the production of this book to ensure that any projects, designs, modifications and/or programs, etc, contained herewith, operate in a correct and safe manner and also that any components specified are normally available in Great Britain, the Publishers and Author(s) do not accept responsibility in any way for the failure (including fault in design) of any project, design, modification or program to work correctly or to cause damage to any equipment that it may be connected to or used in conjunction with, or in respect of any other damage or injury that may be so caused, nor do the Publishers accept responsibility in any way for the failure to obtain specified components.

Notice is also given that if equipment that is still under warranty is modified in any way or used or connected with home-built equipment then that warranty may be void.

About this Book

Computer networks are more commonplace in the home and the workplace nowadays than most people realise. It's not only the large multinational organisations, with their vast IT budgets, that can gain the significant benefits from networking equipment together — the power a network can bring, even in the home environment, far outweighs the relatively low cost (in today's standards) of its implementation.

Obvious benefits are those of device sharing. When you have a good networking solution in place, you can easily connect as many computer devices as necessary to a single peripheral. Devices, such as printers, are fully connectable, reducing the cost of buying additional printers as you add more computers to your environment. The introduction of a network removes the pain of manually moving data around from system to system, as you need to process it on a peripheral device.

This book will explain how to go about planning and setting up a physical network infrastructure in your home or small business, using modern networking technologies (both wired and wireless), and will focus on the best practices of networking professionals to ensure your system is robust, complete and secure.

Many operating systems exist that might be classified network-ready. It would be impossible to cover the configuration and exploitation all of them inside a single volume, so instead, we've concentrated on the most popular home and small business desktop operating system on the market: Microsoft Windows XP. We will explain how to use Windows XP to create a fully featured networking capability for device sharing, Internet connection sharing, file sharing, centralised management and resilient, secure storage.

The book concludes with a look at PC networking security.

Conventions

Throughout this book, you will see a number of information boxes, bounded with either a double line like this...

===

DESIGNATING A WARNING

===

...or indeed, a single line, like this...

DESIGNATING A NOTE, POINT OF INTEREST OR USEFUL TIP

Procedures and walkthroughs are shown as numerical lists, like this:

1. Step 1
2. Step 2

All diagrams and Figures have a two-digit reference number containing the chapter number, followed by the Figure number within that chapter. For example, Figure 1-1 represents the first Figure in Chapter 1.

About the Authors

Tony Campbell has been an IT security consultant, specialising in designing secure systems for government and commercial clients for the last fifteen years. Over the course of his career, he has been exposed to many aspects of the industry and gained considerable experience in both the practical side of IT systems integration and the written side in the production of documentation, technical papers and contributions to monthly journals, such as the Microsoft Windows XP: the Official Magazine, and Windows XP Answers. He has also authored a number of other IT books on server side technologies and networking.

Tony's IT career began in the UK Meteorological Office where he worked as an application programmer before becoming a systems developer. Later he moved into infrastructure engineering before rising to the illustrious level of systems architect. Recently he has consulted to many large IT Services organisations as well as providing consultancy into the small business marketplace.

Tony lives in Hampshire with his wife, Sharon and their daughter Lara

Andrew Edney has been an IT consultant for over 10 years and over the course of his career has worked for a range of high-tech companies, such as Microsoft, Hewlett Packard and Fujitsu Services. He has a wide range of experience in virtually all aspects of Microsoft's computing solutions, having designed and architected large enterprise solutions for government and private sector customers. Over the years, Andrew had made a number of guest appearances at major industry events, presenting on a wide range of Information Systems subjects, such as an appearance at the annual Microsoft Exchange Conference in Nice where he addressed the Microsoft technical community on Mobility Computing. Andrew is currently involved in numerous Microsoft beta programmes, including next generation Windows operating systems, next generation Microsoft Office products and actively participates in all Windows Media Center beta programmes. On top of all of this, Andrew runs his own IT consulting company, Firebird Consulting.

Andrew lives in Berkshire with his partner, Katy, and their two cats.

Acknowledgements

We would like to extend our heartfelt thanks to our family and friends for their support and assistance during the long months of writing this book. In addition to the people explicitly named below, we would also like to extend our thanks to all the staff at Babani for publishing our book.

Primarily, thanks must go to our respective families for being as understanding as they could possibly have been once again when we worked away on our laptops in an attempt to make this book as useful and practical as possible. Thanks to Sharon and Katy for their support and thanks to Lara and our four respective cats for stopping us dragging our hair out when tensions ran high.

A special thanks also goes to Katherine James at Symantec and Emma Ap-Thomas at Red Consultancy, both for providing some software that we used in the book.

To anyone we might have missed, a heartfelt thanks goes out to all of you for making this possible. It's been a pleasure.

Trademarks

Microsoft, **Windows** and **Windows XP** are either registered trademarks or trademarks of the Microsoft Corporation.

All other brand names and product names used in this book are recognised as trademarks, or registered trademarks of their respective companies.

Contents

PART 1
Networks – An Introduction

1

Network Origins

Computer networks have been around for a lot longer than people realise.

The first conceptual idea of a computer came from the imagination of a German aeronautical engineer called Konrad Zuse, back in 1936. He had been trying to solve an engineering problem whereby lengthy and extremely complicated mathematical calculations used in aircraft design often resulted in weeks of wasted effort, and in most cases, that wastage was largely due to human error.

Being a clever and resourceful fellow, Mr. Zuse pondered the problem, and in a flash of brilliance came up with the rudimentary design of the worlds first mechanical calculator, cryptically dubbed the Z1 (see Figure 1-1). Not long afterwards, Zuse prototyped the Z1 and created a fully working model. He then used his invention to solve his longstanding mathematical problem, and it worked a treat.

Figure 1-1 The first mechanical calculating machine, known as the Z1

From Then Until Now

By the beginning of the 1950s, computer manufacturers were producing tangible computer products rather than the scientific prototypes of the previous decade and with the worldwide reach many of these companies possessed, the possibilities and power computers could bring to businesses were beginning to make industry leaders sit up and take note.

The development of computer systems accelerated during the 1960s when most of todays biggest and most well known IT companies (such as International Business Machines — IBM) emerged as pioneers of this computer revolution.

In parallel to the massive private sector push to get computers productised was an initiative run by the US government research agency, Defense Advanced Research Projects Agency. DARPA was looking for ways to enhance and exploit telecommunications networks for the purposes of enhancing defence systems.

In 1969, they successfully demonstrated the very first inter-network (a network of networks) in their research labs — this effectively being the great grandfather of today's Internet. These developments allowed computer systems to communicate over previously unattainable distances using standard telephone cables.

At this point, the two industries — computers and telecommunications — were set on a collision course that would eventually lead to today's Internet connected world.

Back then, it would have been hard to believe that these experiments would change the face of the world, as we know it. However, it was the foresight of a few visionaries of the time that took these networked computer systems to the next level, making them accessible to everyone on the planet, not just the big businesses, education facilities and defence customers.

A brand new, start-up company, run by a programmer called Bill Gates, developed the world's first IBM-compatible

PC operating system, finally making PCs accessible to the public. The company was Microsoft and the product was MS-DOS.

By 1985, the first Microsoft Windows system was rolling out across the United States of America, and people were smitten with the PC bug.

In many cases, the academic community led the way, networking entire campuses together to enable students to use the facilities for both work and socialising with colleagues and friends. Facilities, such as bulletin boards, offered students online communities where people could meet, chat or simply hang out in cyberspace. These systems have now evolved into the multimedia Internet facilities, better known today as Newsgroups and Chat Rooms.

As the Internet grew and the word spread, it became apparent that this new phenomenon was here to stay. Bill Gates suddenly announced an unprecedented change of focus for his company, Microsoft, whereby all future development would be focused on the connected world of the Internet.

We haven't looked back.

Where we are Today

Today, the Internet is available to almost every home and business owner in the UK, with a range of connection speeds available depending on your geographical location and local exchange modernisation.

High-speed connections are available at a relatively low cost in most residential areas and in most places, where telecommunication systems are not up to the task, other methods of obtaining an Internet connection (such as wireless and satellite) are available.

Telecommunication companies are largely responsible for providing the trunk for all Internet backbone communications, with most connections in the home and small business being services over existing telephone lines.

Public libraries offer free Internet access services for their members, allowing anyone to obtain the services of the World Wide Web if required. Broadband connections, multiplexing telephone calls and Internet data connections on a single telephone line, allow the telecommunications companies to exploit the infrastructure they have already invested in, meaning the Internet is readily available to anyone with a telephone at very low cost.

Networking: What's the Big Deal?

For many years, the Microsoft operating system platforms have been able to exploit the services of network connectivity. The latest operating systems that comprise the Microsoft Windows XP family are capable of easily leveraging all modern networking solutions, allowing you access to the rich set of information resources available on the Internet seamlessly and securely. However, the key to successful networking is ensuring you effectively plan your network, understand the requirements and delve a little deeper that the simple Wizard interfaces of Windows XP can offer.

By properly planning and designing your network, you will be able to obtain the best advantage from any existing hardware and software you might already own, as well as attaining the best guidance you need in selecting the right equipment to buy for enhancing your system. You will need to decide which devices you want shared on the network, such as printers and scanners, as well as deciding how network users might share your connection to the Internet.

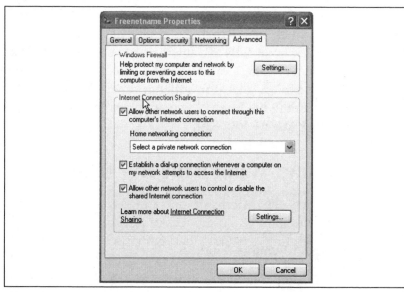

Figure 1-2 The Internet Connection Wizard is easily configured with a single mouse click

Microsoft Windows XP has a built-in facility known as Internet Connection Sharing. The computer you select to use as your ICS host (easily configured through the networking interface on Windows XP, see Figure 1-2) acts as the gateway to the Internet for all other networked computers. Network configuration using the ICS is detailed in Chapter 6.

Plan, Plan, Plan

Before you start wiring things together, you will first need to ask yourself a few questions to aid you in the design process. Obtain a notepad and pen and start sketching where, in your house or office environment, you might want to position your devices. How many computers do you intend to connect to the network? Where will they be located — all in the same room, or scattered all over the place? Are they all desktop PCs, or do you need a few laptops in there as well? What about hardware — do you already own any network equipment you can reuse? To better visualise your network, sketch on your floor plan the location of every electrical and telephone socket and mark any problem areas you notice, such as awkward cable runs that pass through the bathroom. Try joining the devices on the drawing by tracing cable runs through the rooms you need to wire up. This will give you a feeling of how complicated the physical aspect of your network implementation will be.

> The computer acting as your ICS host will need to connect to your Internet access point. This could be your telephone wall socket or a cable television box.

Planning your network should be no different to planning any other kind of DIY job. You will need to Figure out what components you need, then decide how to best connect them together — taking into account any potential pitfalls and looking in details at the risks.

For example, when you install a new radiator, it is important to look at the floor and determine if there will be any obstacles beneath the surface before you pull up your floorboards and ruin your carpets. Networks pose the same kind of problem: if your network is contained within the walls of a single room, cabling is easy, but if it is to span your entire house, you need to plan each cable run carefully. You need to make sure your cable runs are possible; concrete walls, existing electrical appliances, etc, are all hazards that can wreck your plans.

> Good planning really is the key to your success. Tedious as it may seem, it is imperative you make those diagrams and plan those cable runs.

What's on the Horizon?

There are plenty of innovative networking products (hardware and software) on the marketplace that take advantage of your existing physical network. Groundbreaking new software systems, such as Skype (http://www.skype.co.uk) — offering free worldwide phone calls using point-to-point IP connections over the Internet — take full advantage of the Internet infrastructure already in place. Moreover, innovations in hardware technologies, such as Wi-Fi equipment, means these technologies are now coming of age with the introduction of the latest security mechanism — known as Wireless Protected Access (WPA). Users of wireless networks can finally rest easy, content their data is secure. WPA is now widely adopted in both the private sector and in government, underpinning countless new wireless installations that previously would have been impossible using older security protocols, such as Wired Equivalent Privacy (WEP).

This is great news for you since home and small business networks are simplest to install when there are no wires involved. Make sure to check any prospective Wi-Fi purchases for their use of the WPA protocol before proceeding to the checkout.

Summary

From this chapter you can see how important it is to get a basic understanding of what a network is before embarking on an exercise of trying to build and configure one. That is exactly what this book will do for you.

Next, you will learn more about the details of Local Area Networks (LAN), such as the one in your office, and Wide Area Networks (WAN), such as the Internet. You will see the benefits of each and gain an understanding of what the difference between peer-to-peer and server-centric networking is.

You'll go on to be introduced to wireless networking, a relatively new standard in cable-free networking, that can help position computer systems in awkward or mobile environments (for example using a PDA in a warehouse or moving a laptop from room to room in your house).

Finally, you will learn about network security and exactly why security is such a hot topic in today's media.

2

What is a Network?

There is no doubt about it, networks are complicated, especially when you try and equate what's happening at the lowest level (tiny electrical voltages flying around lengths of cable at the speed of light) with the more logical and personable services offered for example on the Internet, such as buying a DVD or a book from Amazon.co.uk.

The trick to understanding how one thing relates to another is to start at the bottom and work your way up. To help with this visualisation, in 1984, the International Organisation for Standardization (ISO) created a framework for defining network architectures, splitting the entire bottom-to-top solution into seven distinct and separate layers. This model, known as the Open System Interconnection or OSI Model, is the most widely accepted method for describing network architectures today.

However, before we delve into the details of the OSI model, let us take a step back and look at the electrical characteristics of a network connection and how we convert the voltages on the a cable into computer readable data.

From Volts to Data

In the same way that radio operators used Morse Code to send messages before, during and after the war, networks communicate using a similar binary language over a similarly analogue medium.

A .-	B -...	C -.-.	D -..
E .	F ..-.	G --.	H ....
I ..	J .---	K -.-	L .-..
M --	N -.	O ---	P .--.
Q --.-	R .-.	S ...	T -
U ..-	V ...-	W .--	X -..-
Y -.--	Z --..	1 .----	2 ..---
3 ...--	4 ....-	5	6 -....
7 --...	8 ---..	9 ----.	0 -----
Stop .-.-.-	Comma --..--		

Table 2-1 Morse Code represented by dots and dashes

Morse Code uses a combination of dots and dashes to represent the characters being transmitted over the chosen medium (see Table 2-1), with each character being transmitted sequentially, and the operator translating each character into English as the message slowly arrives. Representation of the 26 letters of the English alphabet, numerals 0 through 9, and any special characters required to construct the message, is achieved by encoding the character into the appropriate binary pattern then transmitting it over the chosen medium (see Figure 2-1).

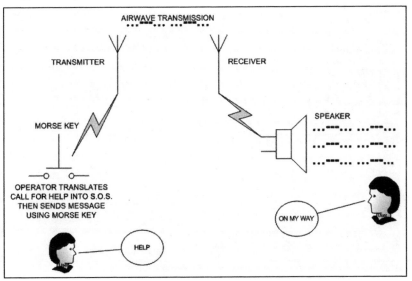

Figure 2-1 Logical flow of Morse Code

Instead of using the audible dots and dashes necessary for the Morse Code operator to hear, computer networks use analogue voltage fluctuations on a cable to represent the binary language understood by computers: translated into numerical binary (base 2) as 1s and 0s.

In an Ethernet Local Area Network (more detail on this later) light-speed voltage fluctuations from the at-rest voltage position (the carrier voltage) on the cable represents the binary numbers of 1s and 0s. A positive voltage fluctuation above the carrier amplitude represents a 1 and a negative voltage fluctuation beneath the carrier voltage represents a 0, see Figure 2-2.

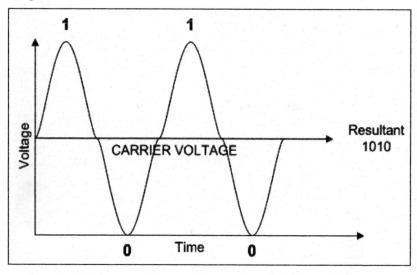

Figure 2-2 Voltage fluctuations represent the binary language of computers

Bits and Bytes

To take the Morse Code analogy one stage further, it is important to understand the basis of how binary voltage fluctuations are converted into comprehensible computer data.

However, before you begin there are two terms that must be properly explained to allow the further explanation of network communication in the correct context. These are bits and bytes.

Bit

A bit is the fundamental building block of all digital communication. The term is derived from the phrase '*B*inary Dig*it*' and represents a single binary digit, either a 1 or a 0.

Byte

A byte is an eight-digit binary number used to represent the code for any single character. The term comes from a contraction of the phrase '*B*inary *T*erm' and consists of eight binary digits, for example 10001000.

> Binary arithmetic is fairly straightforward once you understand the basic principles.

The eight-digit byte is the basis of all network communication and forms the fundamental unit of computer speak.

> A byte has 256 different combinations (from 00000000 to 11111111).

Building Characters, the ASCII way

In the same way that Morse Code can be used to transmit words and sentences by sending a series of dots and dashes, characters being transmitted over computer networks are encoded into binary, with each individual character being represented as a single byte. These bytes are sent over the wire as voltages fluctuations (representing the binary forms of 1 and 0) and are then collected together at the far end of the connection and split into groups of eight (a byte). The receiving computer then translates these bytes into readable characters.

Encoding and decoding the characters relies on a shared understanding of the encoding mechanism, the standard known as American Standard Code for Information Interchange, or ASCII. The ASCII standard splits the 256 available combinations of characters possible with the eight-bit byte into blocks of 32, with each block representing a predefined group of printable characters or control codes. The standard set of ASCII characters takes up half of the byte, from the 0 position through to position number 127.

> Control codes are special characters that perform functions on readable characters, necessary for presentation and formatting. Examples of control characters are carriage returns and line feeds.

ASCII codes 0 to 31

> These codes are special control characters used to perform functions such as Carriage Return (00001101), Line Feed (00001010) and Back Space (00001000).

ASCII codes 32 to 63

> This set of 32 characters comprises more familiar symbols and characters, such as your standard punctuation marks, comma (00101100) and the numbers from 0 through 9.

ASCII codes 64 to 95

> This set of ASCII characters is reserved for all the uppercase alphabetic characters and six special characters, such as the @ symbol (01000000).

ASCII codes 96 to 127

> The fourth and final group of reserved characters comprises 26 lower case alphabetic characters, five special characters (such as braces {}) and a final reserved control character, delete (01111111).

That completes the ASCII standard set. Other standards exist, such as a 16-bit standard called Unicode that significantly extends the character set beyond the 127 characters of ASCII. Unicode remains compatible with ASCII and can be used alongside with few compatibility issues.

> For more information on ASCII and Unicode compatibility, see http://www.unicode.org

Networking Protocols

In order for computer systems to communicate effectively, they need to all speak the same language; voltage fluctuations need to be consistent, the duration of each pulse needs to be understood by all connected hosts and most important of all, there needs to be an agreed etiquette.

The amalgamation of these formalities into a single accessible agreement is called a protocol, and in the computer world, everything that communicates relies on protocols. For the purposes you will be exposed to the two most important protocols in use today: Ethernet and TCP/IP.

Ethernet

Practically every Local Area Network environment you could conceive will use a protocol known as Ethernet for device-to-device communications. Ethernet is a hardware level protocol that determines the characteristics of how devices physically connect.

The Ethernet protocol standard first emerged from the Xerox Corporation's Palo Alto Research Center (PARC) as a way of connecting a computer system to a printer, but this capability soon got the inventive scientists of Xerox further thinking of how they could use such a system.

Today, the Ethernet protocol defines exactly how electrical signals are transmitted across the wires (or wireless) from one computer system to another using an underlying method known as CSMA/CD.

Carrier sense, multiple access, with collision detection

CSMA/CD might sound like a university graduate's dissertation study, but it's actually not that complicated to understand — for your purposes, it is all you really need to know.

CSMA/CD is a protocol and like any other, it ensures all devices respect each other's rules when sending data.

So, what happens when one computer tries to speak to another? On the wires (or airwaves), the sending computer will listen to see if any other machines are trying to chat. This is the *carrier sense* part. If there is already a conversation taking place between some other computers (*multiple access*), the machine attempting to communicate waits, listening to the line until there is a break. When the line becomes free, the sender tries to send its information. If all goes well, a communication channel is established and everyone is happy. However, what happens if another machine attempts to speak at exactly the same time? The answer is *collision detection*. Collision detection forces the systems trying to send information to back off for a random amount of time. This random amount of time is crucial to making this system work. Think about it this way: if you are having a telephone conversation with someone and you both try to speak at the same time, you will probably pause, waiting to see what happens. If the other person does not speak, you say your piece. This random element means both computers should not try and restart the process again at exactly the same time, so, chances are, next time one of them will succeed.

> The principles of the CSMA/CD protocol apply in wired and wireless networks.

As technology has advanced significantly over the years allowing Ethernet systems to operate at higher and higher speeds, cabled solutions can drive data transmission rates up to 1000000000 bits per second.

Most networking infrastructures end up using a combination of transmission speeds, with some devices limited to 10 Mbps, while others might operate at 100 Mbps or even 1 Gbps.

Most modern PC systems come already supplied with an Ethernet compatible Network Interface Card (NIC) in the chassis. It is extremely unlikely if you purchased a brand new PC, especially as a package from a high street retailer, that the system would come without an Ethernet LAN NIC.

Introducing TCP/IP

Most people who have a computer will have at least heard of TCP/IP: but what really is it? Yet another acronym to learn, it stands for Transmission Control Protocol/Internet Protocol and is the industry networking standard used most widely today.

Unlike Ethernet, which is a physical protocol, governing how electrical devices communicate, TCP/IP operates at a higher, more abstract, level, allowing applications to transmit data to each other without worrying so much about the physical characteristics.

Other networking protocols also exist, but with the advent of the Internet (which is solely based upon the services provided by TCP/IP) and the industry standardising development on the paradigm of 'Internet readiness', it's little wonder TCP/IP is removing all competition.

The protocol is designed as a global language, capable of routing many networks together over a number of different connection types (dial-up through to the high speeds of some modern SDSL connections).

Microsoft Windows platforms all rely on the underlying principles of TCP/IP to create their networked environments, and many of the services you rely on in the modern world, such as email and the Internet, would not exist in the way we have come to rely on them without TCP/IP.

The standards for TCP/IP are published as open source documents on the Internet in the format of ratified documents known as Request for Comments (RFCs). These RFCs detail the workings of every underlying TCP/IP service and can be used by system developers when they are creating new applications or operating systems that need to interoperate within a TCP/IP environment.

Standards and Governance

Now that you understand the basic principles behind the transmission of data over a network using voltage fluctuations to render characters, it's time to take a look at the governing bodies that control these standards and set the guidelines for future development.

The development of networking standards for hardware devices and associated protocols falls to a number of governing bodies that, although they are not the owners of the technology in question, they have the academic expertise to set the standards for industry. If companies adhere to these standards they will at least be developing globally acceptable products that will happily interface with other manufacturers' equipment.

To understand the governance hierarchy of the organisations behind these standards, you can focus on the Internet as the largest network on the planet to see exactly what's what and who's who.

> The Internet relies on a protocol known as TCP/IP. You will cover the details of TCP/IP later, but for now it's sufficient to say it's the language of the Internet, and in most cases the language of all modern LANs and WANs.

IETF

The Internet Engineering Task Force is the main governing body that looks after all things Internet related. It is a worldwide community of academic and business experts who contribute to an extensive improvement programme directed at the Internet and all networking services it serves.

The IETF is probably best known for its RFC (request for change) programme, targeting the underlying protocols of the Internet that comprise the TCP/IP suite. These RFCs are submitted to the IETF board for review, are commented on over time by a range of industry and academic experts and eventually, if the change is deemed an improvement to the protocol, it becomes ratified and released as part of the evolving standard.

For more information on the work of the IETF or to view the current list of RFCs that make up the substance of the TCP/IP protocol and Internet set of services, you can visit the website at http://www.ietf.org.

ICANN

The Internet Corporation for Assigned Names and Numbers is an international organisation responsible for the allocation and control of IP addresses. ICANN is directly responsible for the Top Level domain naming system (DNS), whereby it governs the usage of country codes, such as .UK and .AU as well as the delegation of DNS services beneath this level to respective local organisations, such as Nominet in the UK (see http://www.nominet.org.uk).

For more information on what ICANN is doing in the world of governance and standards, take at look at their website at http://www.icann.org.

The OSI Model

There is no doubt in anybody's mind, networks are complicated, and especially if you try to Figure how those tiny electrical voltages in the cables translate to a secure credit card purchase from Amazon.co.uk.

To try to make things a little easier, in 1984, the International Organization for Standardization (ISO) created a framework that defined standard network architectures, splitting the total solution over seven separate layers. This model is called the Open System Interconnection (OSI) Model, or OSI Model for short.

Although network architects and developers use the OSI Model to construct their products, for now, we will concentrate on using the layers purely as a teaching aid to try and help explain the relationship voltages have to what we see on our screens. Each level of the OSI Model can be evaluated in its own right without the need to look above or below. By putting the whole stack together, you build the stack that defines the interfaces at each stage.

From an Internet perspective, the OSI Model was used to define the initial stack for the Internet protocol, known as TCP/IP (Transmission Control Protocol/Internet Protocol).

Stack Definitions

The following list shows the OSI Model's stack layers from the from the ground up:

Physical (Layer 1)

The physical layer, right at the bottom of the stack, represents all aspects of your network that might be considered physical. It defines all electrical and mechanical characteristics of the devices and fully describes the voltages used on the cables, the cables themselves, all your cable connectors and your NICs. From an information perspective all this layer is capable of understanding are the voltages transmitted on the wire. At this point, there is no concept of data, just electricity.

Data Link (Layer 2)

This layer takes you one stage further towards a connected system. It relies on the components provided in Layer 1 to begin interpreting the voltages passed through your cables into some form of communication. This layer is where the MAC address (see the section later in this chapter on the MAC address) is used to identify each system trying to communicate. Some rudimentary error checking takes place in this part of the stack.

Network (Layer 3)

The Network layer provides all the elements of switching and routing needed for your systems to talk to other networks. This layer allows your LAN to be connected to the Internet so you can send email and publish your web site. A comprehensive regime of error checking is also mandated at this stage of data transmission.

Transport (Layer 4)

This layer adds to the error checking regime described in Layer 3 and ensures that all data is sent seamlessly from end system to end system. This means you are guaranteed complete data transfer.

Session (Layer 5)

Here you are beginning to see elements of the network that actually interact with the end user. This layer establishes and manages all system-to-system connections for specific applications. Specific aspects of each application trying to establish a connection with another application are handled here.

Presentation (Layer 6)

This layer is used to provide extra aspects of data formatting, such as encryption, by negotiating the data syntax between the application and the network format. It effectively transforms data into the correct form for the application layer.

Application (Layer 7)

This layer is the key in providing application support to all your system's processes. User authentication is done at this level and elements of privacy are negotiated. This layer provides services for file transfers, electronic mail and web browsing.

More on TCP/IP

TCP/IP is by far the most popular network protocol available today. As already stated, it forms the basis of all communications on the Internet, from web surfing to gaming.

The popularity of TCP/IP comes from the fact that it is so accessible and well controlled, as well as being extensible between LANs and WANs. It offers every capability required to provide maximum flexibility in any size of network.

Microsoft has adopted TCP/IP as the standard protocol for all Windows-based systems, all as part of the Internet ready paradigm adopted by the company in the 80s.

This is best demonstrated when you first run through the installation routines for Windows XP; TCP/IP is automatically installed as the main networking protocol.

The basic principal of a TCP/IP network is that every computer needing to communicate on the network (host) must be configured with its own unique IP addresses. This allows the network to operate in a similar way to the postal service. When one computer wants to send some information to another, it looks up the address of the recipient then sends the information to that destination.

Domain Naming System

Since IP addresses are fairly obscure and don't mean much in the real world, for example, 192.168.9.1, computers use a name resolution service to allow a plain-language version of the computer name to be used instead. This lookup service is called the Domain Naming System or DNS for short. Using DNS, you can send information to addresses such as www.microsoft.com without having to know the numerical equivalent IP address.

A Quick Look in Windows XP

Looking at the TCP/IP configuration dialog for the first time on a Windows XP system can be quite daunting. Plenty of new acronyms to get your head around, and plenty of data fields requiring information.

So, to try and help explain some of these things a little better, we'll jump right in and look into the guts of the system.

1. Click on the Start menu then select Control Panel

2. Double-click on Network Connections.

3. Right-click on the connection icon (shown in Figure 2-3) then choose Properties.

4. Highlight Internet Protocol (TCP/IP) (shown in Figure 2-4) then click on Properties.

This displays the applet that allows you to configure your TCP/IP settings. Most dial-up connections use a system called DHCP to obtain an IP address automatically from the ISP.

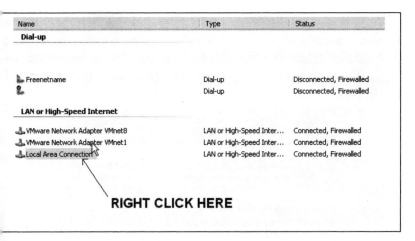

Name	Type	Status
Dial-up		
Freenetname	Dial-up	Disconnected, Firewalled
	Dial-up	Disconnected, Firewalled
LAN or High-Speed Internet		
VMware Network Adapter VMnet8	LAN or High-Speed Inter...	Connected, Firewalled
VMware Network Adapter VMnet1	LAN or High-Speed Inter...	Connected, Firewalled
Local Area Connection	LAN or High-Speed Inter...	Connected, Firewalled

RIGHT CLICK HERE

*Figure 2-3 Right-click on the network
connection icon to get the properties*

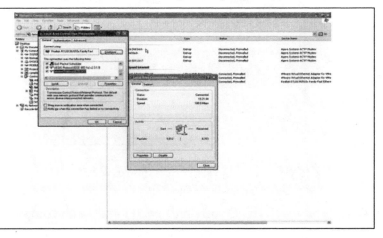

*Figure 2-4 Obtain the TCP/IP properties from
the connection dialog box*

You will see (as shown in Figure 2-5) that this system is set to "Obtain an IP address automatically". This means that DHCP (Dynamic Host Configuration Protocol) is being used to allocate an address to this connection from a central reserve of addresses.

Figure 2-5 This connection is set to use DHCP
to obtain its IP address from a central reserve

When you use DHCP, you don't need to set each computer up and manage the addresses; the system does it for you. The main problem with this interface is that the dialog box does not show you what the IP address allocated to the machine actually is — all you know is it is dynamically allocated. A quick and easy way of viewing a computers actual TCP/IP properties is to run what's called a "command prompt" and use the IPCONFIG utility.

1. Click on the Start menu and select Run
2. Then type CMD.EXE and press Return. You will see the command prompt (shown in Figure 2-6).

Figure 2-6 Use the command prompt to get details about each of your TCP/IP connections

3. At the command line enter IPCONFIG/ALL and press return. You will see all your network connections listed in order, with every setting displayed below.

The MAC Address

As well as a unique TCP/IP address assigned to each networking stack, each piece of networking hardware has its own unique address, known as the MAC address.

MAC address is short for Media Access Control address and is a hardware configured address that identifies each active participant in an Ethernet network. In networks, such as might be installed in the home or small office, the MAC address is independent of the communications protocol that resides above it, for example, TCP/IP.

From an OSI model perspective, applications interface with the network through the top application layer while the MAC layer interfaces directly with the networking infrastructure and is represented as a 48-bit hexadecimal number (12 characters).

The MAC address is assigned to each device by the manufacturer, and might look something like this: 00-32-AC-09-27-21.

If you want to see what the MAC address of all NICs in your system are, use the getmac command from the command prompt. From the command prompt type getmac then press return.

Summary

This chapter has introduced you to a number of crucial aspects of networking and given you an idea of what a network comprises. If you plan to implement a successful network, it really is important you understand these fundamental concepts before steaming into wiring things up and configuring software.

The next chapter goes into the detail of what networking components are available today, as well as recommending which of these components best suit your needs in a small networking environment.

You've seen that TCP/IP is somewhat complicated, but you are beginning to navigate around your system and see that finding the information necessary for network configuration is not all that difficult. We'll go into greater detail later, explaining all about TCP/IP addressing and routing, but for now, the main messages to leave this chapter with are:

- Networks are extensible

- TCP/IP is the standard Internet protocol

- You will be using TCP/IP on *your* network

- Standards for networking exist that help control how systems communicate — and these standards help all of us.

PART 2
Building Networks

3

Networking Components

In this chapter, we will look at the various components that could make up your network. These components include the following: the cables you might install, the type and speed of network card, whether or not you are going to use a hub, switch or a router, and what a firewall is and why it is needed.

Cables

If you have a wired network, you need cabling. This is to connect any devices you might have, for example your computer to your cable modem. Even if you have a wireless network, there is a good chance you may have something connected via a network cable.

The cheapest and most common form of home network cabling is known as CAT5 cabling, as shown in Figure 3-1.

Figure 3-1 A CAT5 RJ45 Ethernet cable

CAT5 is an Ethernet cable standard which is defined by the Electronic Industries Association and Telecommunications Industry Association. It is the 5th generation of twisted pair Ethernet cabling.

CAT5 contains four pairs of unshielded twisted copper wire and supports 100Mbs (also known as Fast Ethernet), and has a recommended maximum length of 100m (328 feet).

A slightly newer version, called CAT5e (or CAT5 enhanced) supports 1,000Mbs (also known as Gigabit Ethernet).

The following table (Table 3-1) shows the generations of twisted pair Ethernet cabling.

CAT	USAGE
CAT1	Used for telephone communications, ISDN and doorbell wiring.
CAT2	Used on 4Mbit/s Token Ring networks.
CAT3	Used on data networks for frequencies up to 16 MHz.
CAT4	Used on 16Mbit/s Token Ring networks.
CAT6	Provides performance up to 250 MHz, more than double CAT5 and CAT5e.
CAT7	Draft standard which is proposed to include four individually-shielded pairs inside an overall shield. Designed for transmission at frequencies up to 650 MHz.

Table 3-1 Different categories of UTP cabling in use today

These cables use one wire-pair for transmission in each direction. This means that the "transmit" pair will be connected to the "receive" pair at the other end. When the cables are connected to a switch or a hub, which we will cover later in this chapter, the crossover is done internally to that device.

However, let us say that you have two computers and you wanted to connect them together but you do not have a switch or a hub. What can you do? Well, the answer is simple. You need a special cable called a crossover cable.

A crossover cable swaps the pairs within the cable, which means you do not need any other device to do it for you.

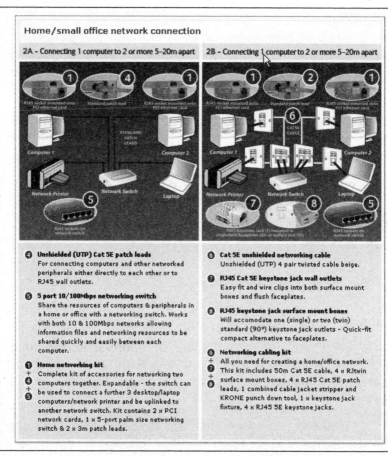

Figure 3-2 A selection of networking kit options available from B&Q's website

Crossover cables are especially useful if you only have a small network, or you want to copy data quickly from one machine to another.

RJ45, or Registered Jack 45, is the physical interface used to terminate the cables. In English, it is the plug-like end of each cable. Of course, you do not have to buy ready made up cables. You could always make your own if you felt daring.

Even your local DIY store probably sells everything you need to wire up your network, including the ability to make your own cables (take a look at Figure 3-2).

Network Interface Cards (NICs)

Network Interface Cards are required if you want to set up any sort of network, be it wired or wireless.

They come in a variety of different formats and speeds and this section aims to help you understand what they are so that you can make an informed decision on what you need for your network.

Each card has its own unique address, known as a MAC (Media Access Control) address. The MAC address is used to direct data to the correct destination.

Wired

Most home or small business networks, if wired is being used, will use either a 10Mbs or a 100Mbs network card in each computer.

Obviously 100Mbs in considerably faster than 10Mbs, however you may not actually need anything faster than 10Mbs, although from a cost perspective you would be wiser going for the faster cards. Besides, it is very difficult these days to actually find a 10Mbs card, as most cards are actually 10/100Mbs switchable. This means that the card will detect the speed of your network and will adjust accordingly.

The type of computer you want to network will decide what type of card you buy.

If you are using a desktop computer, and the motherboard does not have a built-in network card, then you will need to buy a PCI network card. This card will slot into one of the spare PCI slots in your computer and then you will connect the network cable to the port on the back of the card.

Figure 3-3 shows a typical PCI network card.

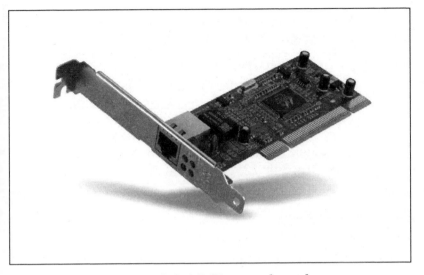

Figure 3-3 A PCI network card

If you are using a laptop computer that does not have a built-in network adaptor, you will need to buy a PCMCIA network card. This will slot into the PCMCIA slot and in turn, you would then connect the network cable to that.

Not everyone however will be able to use a wired network. For example, if you want to network computers in different rooms of your house, but you do not want to run cables everywhere, then you would need to use wireless.

Wireless

Wireless has become so cheap and easy to setup that some computer shops now only carry wireless equipment.

As we have just mentioned, wireless is great if you do not want to have cables all around your home or office.

The most important thing to remember about selecting your wireless equipment is ensuring that what you buy is compatible with anything you already have, for example the speed!

There are many wireless formats available, such as 802.11a, 802.11b, 802.11g, 54g, 125g and so on.

Some of these formats are better than others, and some are now hard to find.

Today, the most common are the 802.11g and 54g formats. Manufacturers such as Belkin, Linksys and others produce networking kit at this format.

For more information on these formats, have a read through Chapter 2 if you have not done so already.

As with the wired cards, wireless cards also come in different varieties.

If you have a desktop computer, you can buy a PCI wireless card. These cards can look, either like a standard PCI network card (but instead of an Ethernet plug on the back, they have an aerial, as shown in Figure 3-4), or they could be a PCI cradle for a PCMCIA card. These can be quite useful as you can use the PCMCIA card on your laptop and then swap it to your desktop if required (assuming you do not want both machines connected to the network at the same time).

Figure 3-4 A PCI wireless network card

If you are using a laptop, and it does not have a built-in wireless adaptor, you can buy a wireless PCMCIA card. As with the wired card, this can be slotted into the PCMCIA slot (see the example in Figure 3-5).

The other option available for both desktop and laptop users is buying a USB wireless adaptor. These are very cheap and again can be used on different devices as long as you do not want to use them at the same time.

Figure 3-5 A PCMCIA wireless network card

Hubs and Switches

A hub is usually used to connect two or more computers on a network.

Hubs can come in a variety of sizes, one of the most popular being 4 ports, see the example shown in Figure 3-6.

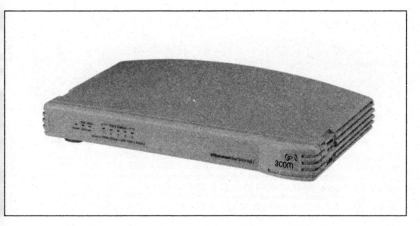

Figure 3-6 A typical small network hub

They are very cheap, quite small, and are very useful to use for connecting a small number of computers on the same network. They just route network traffic onwards and can be used to extend your network.

Switches on the other hand are more expensive, but this is for a good reason. They provide much higher performance than a hub. If you are planning to have more than four computers on your network or you are planning to use applications that generate significant amounts of network traffic, then a switch would be a much better investment.

Switches are also used to divide a network into different segments, see example switch in Figure 3-7.

Figure 3-7 A typical small network switch

Routers

A router is a device that routes data throughout you network, hence the name. Routers act like relay stations; they pass data between points on the journey. Routers are often used to connect your network to another network, such as the Internet via your ISP.

Routers can be both wired and wireless, with even the wireless routers having to have at least one wired connection. An example wireless router is shown in Figure 3-8.

Figure 3-8 A typical wireless network router

Routers often contain additional security settings, such as a firewall and the ability to set up specific routes and settings for your network.

Routers are very cheap and easy to configure.

Firewalls

A firewall is probably the single most important security component you will have on your network. If you do not currently have one, get one now.

Outside of the computing world, a firewall is something that keeps a fire from spreading from one area to the next.

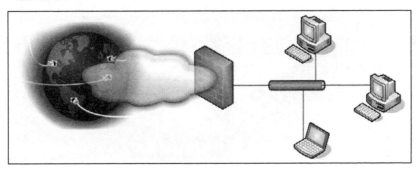

Figure 3-9 A firewall guarding your network

In computing terms, a firewall does the same thing for your network and computers; it filters information coming from another network, such as the Internet, and stops anything from passing onto your network without permission (see Figure 3-9).

A firewall can be a piece of software, such as the Windows Firewall, which is part of the Windows XP SP2 operating system, a product such as the Norton Personal Firewall from Symantec or Personal Firewall Plus from McAfee or even a separate hardware firewall. These are more common in large companies and for the home or small business, a software firewall should be sufficient. More information on the Windows Firewall can be found in Chapter 6. In addition, most wireless routers now come with a firewall built in!

Firewalls can use different methods to control the network traffic passing in or out of your network.

These include:

- **Packet Filtering** – this method examines each packet of data that goes through the firewall and checks it against a set of rules. If there is a rule to allow it, the data will pass through. If not, it is stopped.

- **Proxy** – this method is when the firewall acts as the "middle man". For example, your computer asks the firewall to retrieve information from a website on the Internet, and then that information is passed back to your computer. This means that your computer never actually requests information from the Internet directly.

- **Stateful Inspection** – this method compares certain parts of the packet against a database of trusted information.

Firewall Filters/Rules

Firewall filters, commonly referred to as rules, are a very important component of any firewall.

These are added and removed in order to meet certain conditions, depending on your specific requirements.

> Firewall rules should only be set up to allow what is needed to pass through. The last rule should always be to deny everything.

The rules can include the following:

- IP address
- Domain name
- Protocol
- Port number

The protocol rule is very useful. For example, if you want to allow web traffic through, you just add a rule for the HTTP protocol. These protocols are predefined to make things easier for you.

Table 3-2 lists a number of the more common protocols, along with explanations of what they are used for.

PROTOCOL	EXPLANATION
HTTP	Used for web pages.
FTP	Used for file transfers.
UDP	Used for audio and video, amongst others.
SMTP	Used for email.

Table 3-2 Network protocols and their purpose

What it protects you against

Probably the biggest threat to your network is from either a hacker or a malicious program. Now using a firewall is not a 100% effective deterrent, but it is certainly better than nothing and should stop the average "attack".

> An unprotected computer can be hijacked within minutes of first connecting to the Internet.

Malicious programs come in many forms, including viruses, worms and Trojans. Once a computer has been infected, it can be used without your knowledge. For example, if you use online banking all of your details could be recorded and passed onto someone else!

Summary

This chapter has exposed you to the major components you will use to construct your network and explained their positioning in the bigger picture. You should choose your network components carefully, and where possible seek appropriate advice from your ISP to make sure your devices are compatible. For example, make sure a wireless router that you want to connect to the Internet also has ADSL routing capabilities.

The next chapter goes into a bit more detail on the planning side of networking before launching you into connecting your systems up and configuring them.

4

Planning Your Network

When you finally decide it is time to start planning your network, you need to make sure you take into consideration all aspects of the final installation: cables, hardware, software and indeed, the physical environment. However, before you jump in and starting wiring things together, there are a few more things that need explaining:

- Local Area Networks
- Wide Area Networks
- Wireless Networks

Local Area Networks

A local area network (commonly abbreviated to LAN), is a group of connected computer systems which all share a common communications infrastructure. In every home or small business network, the networking solution will be LAN-based, allowing the sharing of information in a geographically local area, for example, within a warehouse or office environment.

LANs can be configured to provide central resources (known as server-centric), where the governance of communications activity is through a server. Alternatively, they can be set up in a peer-to-peer fashion, where each system manages its own resources with no central governance.

> The majority of home and small businesses LANs are peer-to-peer networking environments. However, many small businesses (over three clients and a server) are now choosing to install server-based technology, such as Microsoft Small Business Server 2003. These solutions rely on the same network architecture as your smaller peer-to-peer solution, however, security governance is controlled centrally by what is known as a Domain Controller (the server).

Peer-to-Peer Networking

Peer-to-peer networks can grow to be as elaborate and complicated as required. However, control of network resources becomes complicated as the network evolves, and can become cumbersome when you reach critical mass. It's advisable that if you intend to have over five client workstations connected to a LAN you think about server-centric networking.

On a small scale, managing the data access permissions on three PCs is straightforward, although, even two machines can begin to create administrative overheads (such as data backups) that you might find annoying. A typical peer-to-peer network is shown in Figure 4-1.

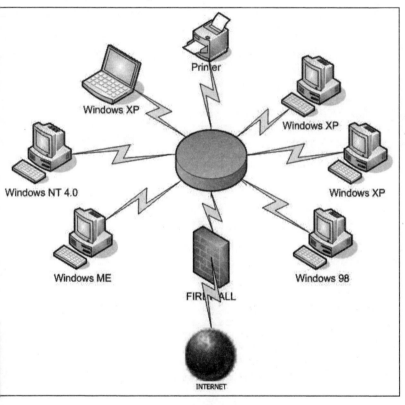

Figure 4-1 A typical peer-to-peer network configuration, featuring six PCs, one printer and an onward Internet connection

In a Windows environment, the peer-to-peer network is known as a Workgroup, and this is how you will set your computers up in relation to this book. A Workgroup is simply a Microsoft networking term that describes a loosely coupled network where security control is devolved to each machine in the federation. You can see in Figure 4-2 where your computer's Workgroup name is defined.

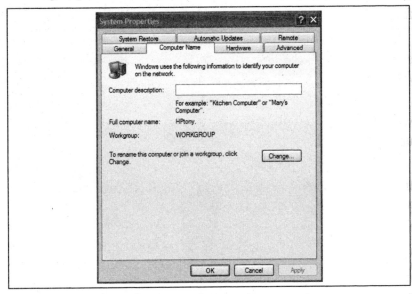

Figure 4-2 In this example, the Workgroup name is still set at the Windows XP default, WORKGROUP

Wide Area Networks

Wiring systems up locally is one thing, but the real power from networking comes from their ability to span long distances.

Communicating with family members or collaborating with your business customers (who might be situated on the far side of the planet) is now commonplace over the Internet.

Making this all possible, you'll be exploiting the services of the world's largest Wide Area Network: *the Internet*.

A wide area network (WAN) connects systems over a wide geographical area, primarily acting as a way of joining up LANs.

To use a real-world analogy of how email flows across the Internet, when you send an email to a family member in another country, the message is composed on your local computer then posted across your LAN, out through your Internet gateway (your dial-up or Broadband router) to your Internet Service Provider. The message is subsequently transmitted through many email relay systems until it finally reaches the recipient's PC on the end of another Internet gateway device, and quite possible on the end of another LAN.

Things to remember about WANs:

- WANs connect LANs together
- WANs are the responsibility of your telecommunications company, normally British Telecom in the UK.

- You have no direct control over the WAN — you simply subscribe to the services provided by them

- The most widespread WAN is the Internet

To get an idea of how distributed the Internet is, have a look at *The Internet Mapping Project* run by Bell Labs in the USA. This project has been running since the summer of 1998 and they have successfully mapped the majority of the extent of the Internet's reach.

Their goal is to analyse the layout of the Internet as it evolves over time, helping with the long-term planning of sizing and distribution. To date, their data has helped fix routing problems and help track down the source of Distributed Denial of Service (DDoS) attacks. For more information, see:

http://research.lumeta.com/ches/map/index.html

Wireless Networking

It was not long ago that wireless networks were not even a consideration by most businesses, let alone home users.

The hardware components were so exorbitantly expensive that the average company's budget could not stretch that far, and coupled with the fact that the technology was so complicated you needed a degree in electrical engineering to understand it, wireless (or Wi-Fi) simply was not an option.

However, that was five years ago; today things are very different. As a result of significant developments by the

Institute of Electrical and Electronic Engineers (IEEE), a standard for wireless networking was ratified in 1999, known in industry as IEEE 802.11. Over the past years, fierce competition in the market has resulted in the simplification of the technology and enormous price drops. Nowadays Wireless Local Area Networks (WLANs) are not only a practicable alternative to copper cabling, they are fast becoming the norm.

Microsoft has made life even easier for Windows users by integrating WAN drivers into Windows XP. WLAN network cards now automatically configure themselves, making it possible for you to install and configure a WLAN system in a matter of minutes. This offers the flexibility of being able to reach the Internet (via your dial-up or Broadband solution) while sitting in front of your favourite TV show with your laptop, or possible from the garage when working on the car.

Planning Basics

Get out your notepad and pen and start sketching your environment, taking into account the answers to the following questions:

1. How many computers do you intend to connect into your network?

2. Where will these systems be located: all in the same room or are they scattered all over the place?

3. Are they all desktop PCs or do you need to network a laptop, printers, etc?

4. What hardware do you already own and what will you need to buy?

To visualise your network, try sketching the floor plan, showing the location of each device you intend to connect. Show every electrical and telephone plug and also mark any problem areas you see, such as cable runs that pass through the bathroom or living room. Join the devices by drawing the cable runs and mark the Windows XP computer thats going to be the ICS host.

Where you see a problem with cable runs, consider using a WLAN connection instead. It might be more cost effective to forget cables altogether and go straight for Wi-Fi.

Which Components go Where?

Now that you are familiar with the components that make up a network, be it a LAN or a WAN (including Broadband and dial-up networks) you should construct a rudimentary network diagram to help plan the installation.

Planning a network is no different to planning any other DIY job. Firstly, Figure out what components you need, then you Figure out how to connect them together.

The key to success is making sure to avoid any problem areas and trying to eliminate complications that could make the final installation more difficult, and potentially impossible.

When you install a new radiator, you look at the floor and determine if there will be any obstacles beneath the surface before you pull up your floorboards. Networks pose similar problems. If the network is to be contained within the walls of a single room, then cabling is much easier to install and hide than if it is to span the entire house.

> Plan each cable run meticulously, and where you might find difficulties or the route is impossible, consider using an alternative technology such as Wi-Fi.

If you have access to a CAD system, try drawing a complete network diagram. This planning diagram will help you when you come to buying cables of the right length.

Create Professional LAN and WAN Diagrams

Have a go at creating professional network diagrams by downloading Pace Software's free 30-day trial of LanFlow Net Diagrammer. This software can be downloaded and used for up to 30 days after which you must pay $89 to keep using it. This will help you to draw LAN, WAN, Network and Phone system diagrams, or any other style of diagram that comprises network devices and interconnections. LanFlow has built-in icons for computers, workstations, servers, routers and hubs and the dynamic connectors represent your cables, wires, power, or even logical communication paths. Look at http://www.pacestar.com/lanflow for more information.

Internet Connectivity

You will need to have an account set up at your Internet Service Provider (ISP) in order to route traffic from your internal network to the Internet. The ISP will be able to provide the following:

- Physical Internet connectivity, such as through your telephone socket

- A connection device, such as an ADSL modem or dial-up modem

- Email accounts

- Web site space

- Domain name resolution (access to a DNS server)

- Advice on specific configuration requirements between your own network and the Internet

When you approach an ISP, check how wide ranging and versatile their service portfolio is. You certainly do not want to be tied into a 12-month contract that prohibits you upgrading from dial-up to ADSL access.

Connection Speeds

The best value for money by far is ADSL 2/2+, giving you an "always-on" Internet connection for roughly the same price as the old dial-up service would have offered.

Obviously, in places where ADSL is still unavailable, (it's all to do with telephone exchange upgrade schedules) then you might have to opt for one of the other methods. The easiest and quickest is to use a dial-up connection. These dial-up connections have been around for a long time and are slow and costly under many service plans. Although the top connection speed is 56 Kbps, this is rarely achieved, and more than likely the modem will connect around 40 Kbps.

Other possible connection types, such as satellite or microwave uplinks are available, and in these cases, you will have exhausted all other routes of enquiry. Sometimes, if the service you are after is unavailable, it's worth asking the ISP or telecommunications company what criteria they would consider might make it worthwhile installing the capability. For example, some companies will wait until they have enough general queries from a particular postcode before upgrading the local exchange. It might be worth canvassing your local area to see if you can get enough interested parties.

Connection devices

Once you have established which Internet Services Provider you are going to use, and decided upon the most suitable connection method, you'll need to work with your ISP to decide upon the best equipment to facilitate that connection.

The choice of equipment depends upon which type of service you've gone for, for example, a dial-up connection requires a traditional modem (one that might be already built into your PC) and telephone line, while a microwave service requires a router, specialised cables and a microwave receiver.

The choice also depends largely on the product set available through your ISP. If you opt for ADSL, for example, you will need a suitable telephone line, a broadband modem and a set of microfilters. Depending on the package you select and the complexity of the connection type, you will either get a DIY installation kit (for dial-up and ADSL), or you'll get an engineer out to set it up.

ADSL microfilters are in-line connection devices that allow you to plug your modem or router directly into your telephone line. They are cheap and normally come as part of the package when you order ADSL. The filters are there as a way of removing the audible data signal from the telephone line.

Email Accounts

When you order your Internet package, be sure to decide how you want to handle email. If you want only a single email for all email users to use, this is cheaper than each user having their own address — but what about privacy? It might be better to buy a package where you get five email addresses you can configure yourself. Do you need access to email when away from your PC? If so, check if the ISP offers a webmail service, where you access your inbox through Internet Explorer.

Planning a Wired Network

A typical small-scale Ethernet network comprises a number of computers, each with their own network interface cards, connected together using Ethernet cables, through the interface ports on hubs or switches.

What Speed is the Network?

Ethernet networking components can operate at a number of different data transmission rates, as discussed in Chapter 2, but the speed the entire network performs at is determined by the lowest common denominator on each connection. If you have a requirement for a high-speed network, choose modern components capable of transmission speeds of at least 100 Mbps and make sure you buy good-quality CAT5e or CAT6 patch cables.

Should you use a Hub or a Switch?

As has already been illustrated in Chapter 3, a switch divides a network into segments, allowing traffic to any individual port to be isolated from the rest of the network. In a small network, the majority of network traffic is directed at the Internet Connection Sharing Host machine, so it makes no sense to choose a switch over a less expensive hub. The only thing to bear in mind is that switches have come down significantly in price and in many cases manufacturer's preference is the switch (some have even stopped producing hubs). If you have no option, then a switch it must be.

How Many Devices do you want to Connect?

Count the number of network devices you want connected to your network: this includes PCs, network printers, wireless uplinks or any other Ethernet device. The total number of hosts will equate to the minimum number of ports you need on your hub or switch. To facilitate expansion and to make sure you have not missed anything, add 25% to the port count.

How many cables and how long?

Measuring the length of a cable is not as straightforward as it sounds. A common mistake is to judge the length of the cable based on the computer's proximity to hub or switch. When you come to feed the cable through cable ducting or under the carpet, you suddenly find you are 50 cm short. This wastes a lot of time and money, and commonly the cable ends up in a bag in the garage, unused, gathering dust.

Planning Wireless

Wireless networks pose their own set of unique planning problems. WLANs use a special kind of hub, known as a Wireless Access Point and the major consideration when planning a WLAN implementation is where best to place the Access Point for uninterrupted radio broadcasting.

Household devices, such as microwave ovens, mobile phones and even electrical cabling can disrupt the performance of the most commonly used Wi-Fi equipment (based on the 802.11b and 802.11g standards).

The most effective place to put an access point is high up, on a plinth, where as many computers as possible have an unblocked, line-of-sight view to the antenna. Try to make sure the access point is as centrally located to all your computers.

Network Security 101

Microsoft has developed a whole range of specialist security utilities that really help you bolster your network defences: all you need to do is know the right way to make best use of them. In addition, you need to understand the problems faced when trying to secure a network, especially from the point of view of the criminals who wish to take advantage of any exposure of your services or systems to the wider world. Connectivity to the Internet is the main problem we all face, and with the advent of always-on Broadband connections, our attack surface (the amount of time and resources available for attacking our systems open to the cybercriminals) has increased exponentially.

Defining Cybercrime

Computer crime, known in the industry as *cybercrime,* is on the increase. Government-run specialist crime units are springing up all around the world in an attempt to tackle the proliferation of the more violent crime, such as online pornography, paedophilia and terrorism, as well as trying to tackle the less violent, yet still destructive rackets, such as illegal gambling, drug distribution and fraud. Police forces are cooperating through international partnerships with other countries to tackle some of the more organised of these global enterprises, but the smalltime criminals are still operating largely untouched.

Cases have arisen where people are coerced into parting with large sums of cash for bogus products, fraudulent lottery tickets and recently, impersonation of legitimate services such as eBay or banks.

Two USA government law-enforcement agencies, the Federal Bureau of Investigation and the National White Collar Crime Center, formed a coalition partnership in May 2000 called the Internet Fraud Complain Center (IFCC), whose goal was to offer businesses and private Internet users some method of contacting an official investigatory body if they suspected they'd been targeted by Internet fraudsters. In the first year they received in excess of 30,000 calls.

In the UK, the best resource for understanding cybercrime, its extent and the authorities' response, is the National Hi-Tech Crime Unit.

NHTCU

In the UK, the National Hi-Tech Crime Unit is a multi-agency initiative set by the Serious Organised Crime Agency to tackle all aspects of large-scale crime in the UK. They also liaise with counterpart initiatives in countries all over the world to combat threats such as bribery, corruption, hacking and illegal drug trafficking, see Figure 4-3. The authorities can be contacted at: http://www.nhtcu.org.

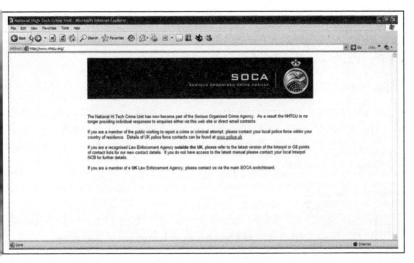

Figure 4-3 SOCA and the NHTCU are fighting cybercrime in the UK

Physical Security

Information and networking security is covered in more detail in later chapters, but for now, it's sufficient to say that in the planning stage you should always be bearing in mind that security is a wider issue than simply antivirus software and a firewall. The final consideration in planning a secure installation is to look at aspects of physical security.

Physical security countermeasures protect your systems from the obvious problems of theft, tampering and espionage.

The following list of threats and their respective countermeasures can be applied in the home or small office to help reduce your risk of data loss:

Exterior Doors

Make sure outer doors are secure, if possible, using deadlocks or alternatively, if your door doesn't have this extent of security at least you should install a chain and bar.

Internal Doors

Make sure all doors leading to I.T. equipment are fitted with a security bolt at the top and bottom of the door.

Windows

All ground-floor windows should be lockable. Alternatively, fix windows shut using internally fitted non-return screws.

Workstations

Use case-locks on all computers. Laptops should be stored in a cabinet or drawer out of sight from windows.

Burglar Alarm

Install a burglar alarm system that connects to the local police force. These systems might be expensive, but the installation cost can be offset against the price of your insurance.

Check Your Hardware Compatibility

As a check before you purchase any additional hardware, it's a good idea to see if items such as network interface cards or Wi-Fi devices are compatible with your Windows XP computers.

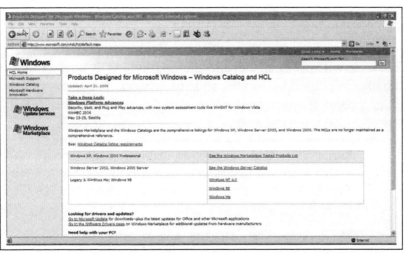

Figure 4-4 Hardware and Software
Compatibility on the Internet

To check if the hardware is compatible, you can look on the online catalogue provided by Microsoft. All the major hardware vendors have supplied their devices for in-depth testing with the Microsoft platforms (including the future implementation with Vista) and if a product passes the stringent tests carried out in the Microsoft labs, they get the seal of approval and listed on the Internet, see Figure 4-4.

The catalogue lists approved hardware and software that has been tested on Windows XP:

http://www.microsoft.com/whdc/hcl/default.mspx

The Simplest Network Ever: One Room, Two Computers

There are only a few things that need considering when your network will not span beyond the confines of a single room. Firstly, you should select the style of network that is easiest for your needs: if your computers already have Ethernet NICs installed, all you need to buy is a single crossover cable.

Remember that crossover cables limit the network to two machines. They are fine in this environment, but if you wish to expand any further, you will need a hub.

Make sure you do not accidentally try to connect crossover cables between a hub and your PC, the connection will fail.

If you do not have any built-in Ethernet NICs, you will need to buy an Ethernet network adapter for each machine, unless you opt to install a WLAN; then you will need some Wi-Fi kit.

USB Ethernet NICs are by far the easiest wired interface cards to install.

Next, you will have to measure the distances from one computer to the other, adding an extra metre or two in case you need to reposition the systems later. Make sure you carefully follow the route you want the cable to take when you measure it as the twists and turns of hiding cables under the carpet or floorboards will undoubtedly add extra length.

You will also need to decide which of your computers will be your Internet Connection Host. One of your computers will connect to the Internet as well as your LAN and act as a gateway for all other computers to access the World Wide Web (see Figure 4-5).

> When you decide which computer will be the Internet Connection Host, contact your ISP to see what hardware you will need for that connection. If you are connecting using DSL then you might have to buy two NICs, one for the ISP connection and another for the LAN connection.

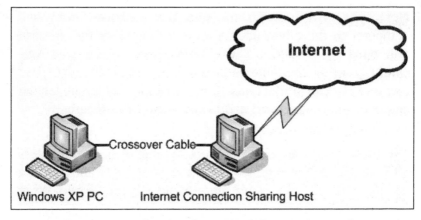

*Figure 4-5 The Windows XP PC connects to the
Internet through the ICS Host*

Expanding Beyond One Room

Firstly, you should realise your network can be as large as you like. It can grow, and grow and grow to whatever size you need — if you need it to span five different buildings, and ten homes, that's not a problem, just not the goal of this book. However, what this book will do for you is enable you to set up a network infrastructure that is extensible and can be built upon if required.

Remember Wireless

If you decide to go for a WLAN then you'll need to get some specialised equipment. You will need an access point to act as the central transmitter/receiver of radio signals between computers and you'll need a wireless NIC for each machine.

Summary

This might seem a peculiar place to stop the planning chapter before moving into the implementation stage. However, if you've followed all the steps in this chapter, you'll have more than enough grounding to tackle any size of installation or any complexity of network requirement.

Case Study

Picture it. The network is expanding, you've got your LAN in your home office with two Windows XP PCs (one for work and one for play), one of them acting as your Internet Connection Sharing Host. Your daughter is happy because she can access the Internet from her room using her wireless system, and the phone carries on working since you installed the Broadband and microfilters. The following weekend, you decide to buy a Media Center PC to play movies downstairs (with a built-in Wi-Fi network). You discover your son also needs to get connected as his new shoot em up provides Internet gaming free of charge and he simply must have it. It is time to expand and completely network the house.

Sounds ominous, doesn't it. However, once you plan it using what you have learned in this chapter, it is easy.

The rest of this book covers the practical wiring up and configuring of your network as well as all the niceties the network will provide, such as file sharing, printer sharing, web surfing, email and gaming.

5

Connecting Everything Together

The next stage is the fun part: wiring it all up. In this chapter, you will learn how to plug in your cables, connect your access points, hook up your microfilters and test what you've installed.

The Best Laid Plans of...

If you followed through the last chapter, you will have already have purchased all the right equipment, measured all your cables, ordered the right package from your ISP and have your network schematics, however rough and ready, in your hand and ready to follow. Now, arrange all your pieces in the rooms where you intend to install them and start systematically working out from the Internet and around the house, PC by PC until you complete the task.

Figure 5-1 shows a typical network schematic consisting of two PCs connected through a hub with one of the PCs acting as an Internet Connection Sharing Host.

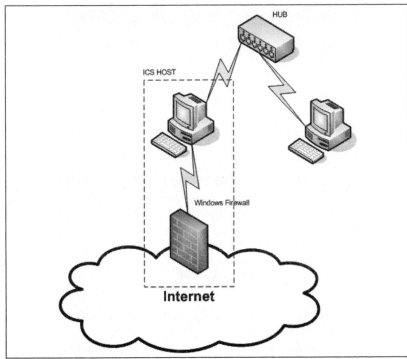

Figure 5-1 Two PCs connected through a hub and out to the Internet via the ICS host

Cabling Techniques

Cabling is straightforward: it is a matter of being meticulous and systematic in your approach, then you should have little problem in getting the right electrical signals to the right connectors, and at the right time.

The main concern is making sure that when you come back to your solution a month, or even a year, later, you understand what you've installed and can easily translate your drawings into the physical world.

A Tidy Installation

Make sure your cables are tidy when you install them. Use cable ties to stop them becoming tangled, and if possible, use cable ducting to contain them.

Cable ties are those small plastic strips that fasten at one end and the other end pulls through to tighten the binding. They come in all sorts of lengths and widths and come in various colours in case you want to separate data and power by colour.

You can buy cable ties and cheap, floor-level ducting from your local DIY shops, such as B&Q or Wicks. Alternatively, you can install professional ducting (available from various specialist suppliers) around your walls, although this is more appropriate for an office than a home network, see Figure 5-2.

Ducting will serve many purposes, not least the following:

- It allows you to separate data cables from power cables so cutting down on interference and data loss

- It keeps messy cables out of sight so your installation looks professional and well thought through

- Extra cable length is hidden inside the trunking, allowing you to over-specify cabling requirements at the planning stage, then you have the flexibility of moving something after installation.

Figure 5-2 Use cable ducting to carry data and power cables in separate compartments

Outlets for your network points and power points can be mounted on the outside of the ducting so that PCs can simply plug into their nearest point.

Patch Panels and Structured Wiring

A structured wiring solution allows you to flood wire your environment, creating as many data outlets as you require, not only now, but also in the future.

If you flood wire a building, you will install many outlets, and in the early stages of implementation only connect to a small number.

Using a piece of hardware known as a patch panel (the patch panel is where all the data outlets are terminated) you will be able to connect together different segments of your solution as you need to

A typical patch panel is shown in Figure 5-3.

If you are installing a patch panel or a structured wiring solution, you should make sure you have a wiring cupboard or dedicated room to house it.

The entire networking infrastructure and your network server could well take up a lot of space, forming the central hub of your network, so for this reason, many people using structured wiring store their servers and networking equipment in the garage (or unused office).

All you will see on the desktop is the client PC and a flying lead to connect to the data outlet. Printers can also be connected to the network using this sort of structured wiring solution.

*Figure 5-3 A typical structured wiring patch
panel*

Many new houses are being built with structured
wiring panels included in the price. The builders are installing
a flood wire solution, with data outlets in every room, and
normally plumbing the television wiring in alongside.
Telephone signals can be carried over the structured wiring
from the BT termination point, allowing you to reroute the
telephone via the patch panel to anywhere you need in your
house.

By inference, this also means your broadband service can also be routed to the same location.

Setting up your Wi-Fi Network

When you install a Wi-Fi network, you will be using a Wi-Fi Access Point to act as the hub for wireless communication for the client PCs with appropriate Wi-Fi network cards.

The Access Point should be placed close to the physical centre of the communications bubble you are trying to create. Imagine a sphere, 100 feet in diameter around your access point – this is your wireless coverage. However, your coverage will almost certainly be affected by physical interference, such as output from a microwave oven, mobile phone usage, CRT televisions, and standard power cables. This means your conceptual sphere now looks a bit shabby and irregular, especially the further you go from the broadcasting centre.

A good rule of thumb is to use half of the broadcasting range, as advertised on the product specification, as your maximum range, and if you need to go any further, link to a second, connected wireless access point, or alternatively use a wired/wireless hybrid network.

You might also be using a wireless router to connect to the Internet. It's possible to remove the need for an Internet

Connection Sharing host system by having a standalone wireless broadband system do this job for you.

*Figure 5-4 The Linksys wireless Broadband
router (picture courtesy of Linksys)*

Take a look at http://www.linksys.com to see what Linksys are offering in the wireless range. Figure 5-4 shows the Broadband router that offers an internal Wireless 802.11 b/g network as well as that onward connection to your Broadband provider, such as British Telecom.

Summary

Cabling a network can be a lot of fun. It's the practical aspect of computing that a lot of engineers really enjoy, and it's certainly a great feeling when you've installed all the hardware, connected all your systems and you finally have all your systems chattering together in the way you want. It's important to plan your cabling installation, and it's important to document what you install for later reference. Finally, being neat, using cable ties and ducting, will help immensely with the ergonomic appeal and safety of your installation.

Next, it's time to start looking at the logical aspects of networking configured through the operating system. The examples used here are using Windows XP Home Edition, however, other operating systems use similar principles and means to provide this functionality.

PART 3
Networking Windows XP

6

Windows XP Networking

This chapter concentrates on the networking capabilities of Windows XP and explores in detail how to configure and analyse the capabilities of Windows XP for providing connectivity and application level collaboration.

A Quick Tour of Network Connections

It's essential that you learn where the configuration of your network will be held, and more importantly, learn where you will be changing it to best suit your needs.

We will start by looking at the Network Connections interface, shown in Figure 6-1.

To access the Network Connections interface, do the following:

1. Click on the Start menu

2. Click on Connect To...

3. Click on Show All Connections

Figure 6-1 The Network Connections interface

The menu options available from this interface are as follows:

Create a new connection

This option launches the New Connection Wizard and allows you to set up and configure a new dial-up or local area connection, depending on which hardware interface you want to connect through.

Set up a home or small office network

This option launches the Network Setup Wizard, a special configuration wizard that automatically conFigures a small network for information sharing and Internet access without the user having to contribute much or understand what is going on under the surface. We will cover this in more detail, however, it's worth delving into the detail so you can troubleshoot your network if things go wrong.

Change Windows Firewall settings

This option brings up the Windows Firewall configuration dialog box and allows you to modify how the Windows Firewall functions with respect to each network interface.

Disconnect this connection

This option is available for dial-up connections that have been connected to an ISP. Clicking this option disconnects it from the ISP and relinquishes the DHCP allocated IP address.

Rename this connection

This option allows you to rename the connection if required. If you have multiple dial-up connections it's worth making sure you name them so they are easily identified from each other.

View status of this connection

This option displays a dialog box that shows more detail about the individual connection. From here you can delve into the low-level configuration of the connection (more later).

Delete this connection

This option is self-explanatory. It deletes the network connection from the Network Connections screen. If you delete a connection the only way to get it back is to run through the New Connection Wizard.

Change settings of the connection

This option displays the connection properties and allows you to perform some low-level configuration on the IP addressing, dialling options, hardware configuration, etc.

This menu may change depending on which network connection you have highlighted, and the underlying dialog boxes and configuration menus may change depending on the nature of the individual connection. For example, if you are using a Wireless network interface card, the configuration dialog box will allow you to do different things to that of a dial-up adapter connection.

The New Connection Wizard

The New Connection Wizard is used to step through the process of defining and configuring connections that your computer can use to communicate through the various connected interfaces.

To start the New Connection Wizard, do the following:

1. Click on the Start menu

2. Click on Connect To

3. Click on Show all connections

4. Underneath the Network Tasks menu, on the left-hand side of the screen, click the "Create a new connection". This starts the Wizard, as shown in Figure 6-2. Click "Next".

Figure 6-2 Click Next to start the New Connection Wizard

5. On the Network Connection Type screen, as shown in Figure 6-3, you will need to decide on the kind of network

connection you are creating. For this exercise we will
select the top option "Connect to the Internet" to
demonstrate the Wizard. The other options are self-
explanatory (or covered in detail later in the book) so they
will not be explored here. When you have selected the
appropriate radio button, click "Next".

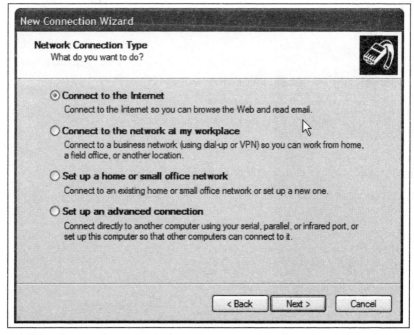

*Figure 6-3 Select Connect to the Internet from
the menu to set up an Internet dial-up
connection*

6. On the Getting Ready screen (shown in Figure 6-4) click on "Set up my connection manually" then click on "Next" to proceed to the next step.

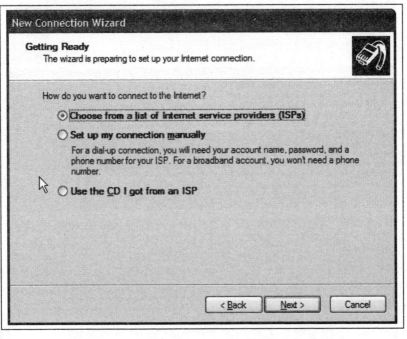

Figure 6-4 Change the radio button from the default to "Set up my connection manually" before clicking "Next"

7. On the following screen, "Internet Connection" you have the choice between a dial-up modem, a fast broadband connection that requires a username and password, or indeed, an always-on connection. For this example, select the topmost menu item, "Connect using a dial-up modem",

as shown in Figure 6-5. When you are ready to proceed, click "Next".

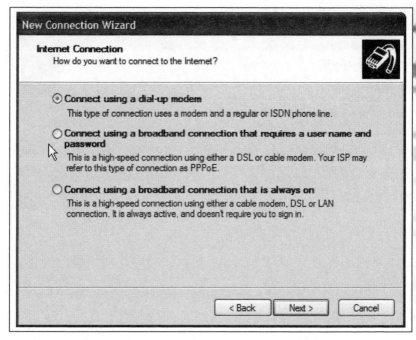

Figure 6-5 Select "Connect using a dial-up modem"

8. The following screen allows you to add a meaningful name to the connection. You have the option, later, if you desire to change this name so don't' panic if you decide you don't like how you've referred to the ISP. This name is only for reference and to identify the connection on the screen, it forms no part of the mechanics of the connection itself. Type the name you choose for this connection in the

blank text-entry field in the dialog box, shown in Figure 6-6 then click on "Next".

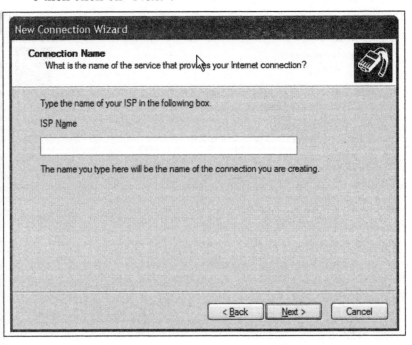

Figure 6-6 Type in a meaningful name for your connection then click on "Next"

9. You will now be requested to type in the telephone number you need to dial to establish connectivity with the ISP's modem, see Figure 6-7. This number will need to be the number you would normally dial to acquire direct connection to an external telephone number, so make sure in a business environment, where you need to dial a prefix to establish an outside line (such as a 9 or a 0), you add

this to the ISP number in this text entry field. So a number might look like this: 90800789789.

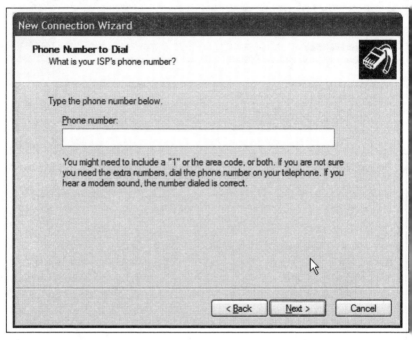

Figure 6-7 Type in the phone number of the ISP making sure you add any prefixes for outside lines if necessary

10. Now you will need to type in the username and password you use to access the remote account on the ISP. This information should have been supplied to you when you set up the ISP connection, but if you are unsure, get in touch with your ISP before typing anything in. If you want this dial-up connection to be used with these login

credentials when any other users use this computer, make sure the checkbox "Use this account name and password when anyone connects to the Internet from this computer" is checked. If this is to be the default Internet connection, make sure you also check the appropriate checkbox. Sometimes, you might have more than one connection identified so you will need to select one of them to be your default. It is most appropriate to have the default connection as the one you use the most. These options are shown in Figure 6-8.

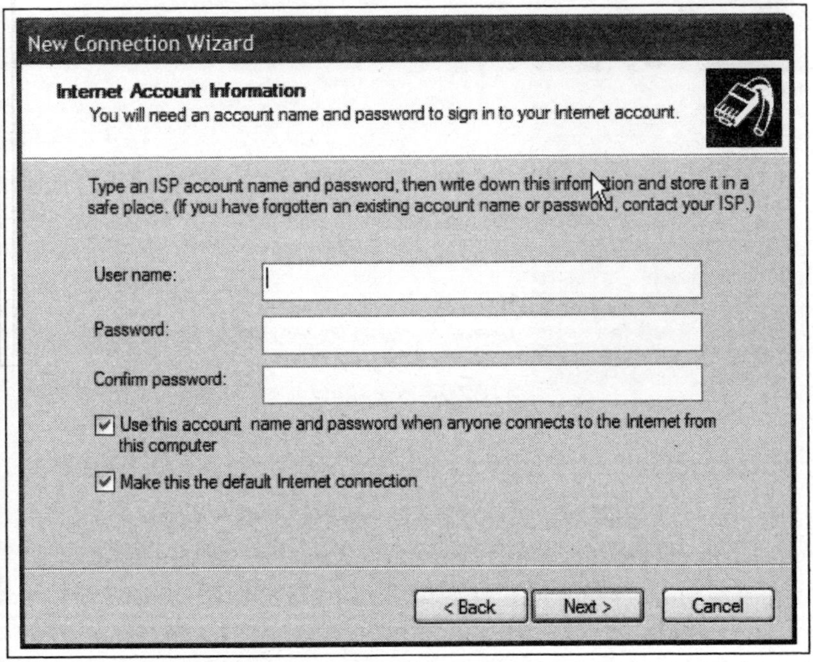

Figure 6-8 Enter the username and password

11. Ok, you are almost done. On the last screen, you can elect to have the wizard create a shortcut to the new connection on your desktop by selecting the appropriate checkbox, shown in Figure 6-9. When you are done, click on "Finish".

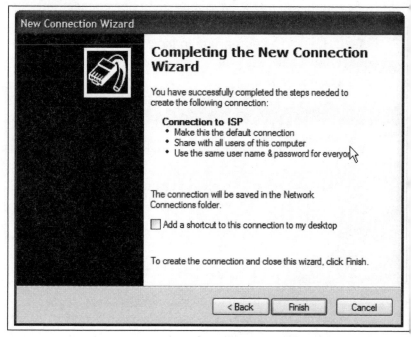

Figure 6-9 Review the settings you entered during the wizard then click "Finish" to create the connection with those settings

The Network Setup Wizard

Take a look at Figure 6-10. The easiest way to set up a small home or business network is to click "Set up a home or small office network" on the Network Tasks menu on the left-hand side of the Network Connections page.

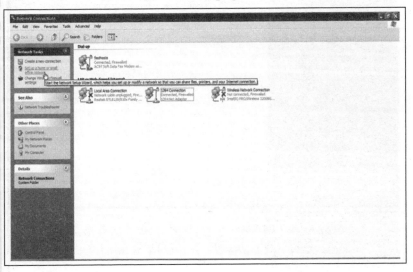

Figure 6-10 Use the Network Setup wizard to create your home or small business network from scratch

When you click this link, the Network Setup Wizard will automatically start, showing the Welcome screen shown in Figure 6-11.

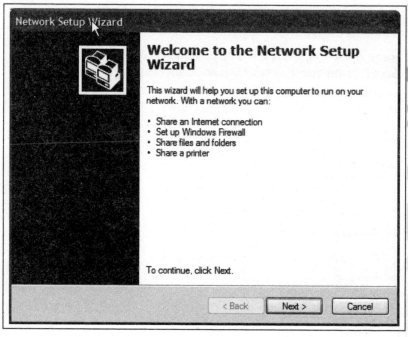

*Figure 6-11 Click "Next" to start configuring
your network using the Network Setup Wizard*

The following walk-through guides you through
successful completion of the Network Setup Wizard:

1. Click "Next" on the Welcome page to start the
   configuration process.

2. The following screen (shown in Figure 6-12) gives you the
   option of clicking the link "checklist for creating a
   network" to see some additional information on network

configuration (see Figure 6-13). When you are ready to proceed, click the "Next" button.

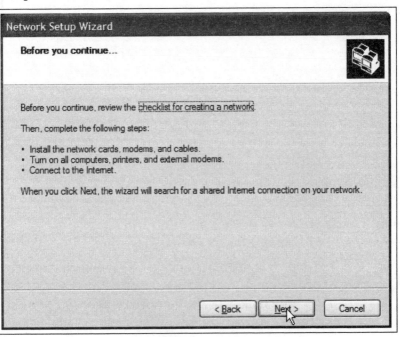

Figure 6-12 Click the link to see a networking checklist before you begin

The network checklist gives you all the information you will need to set up your network. Work through the checklist before proceeding to ensure you have covered all necessary configuration items.

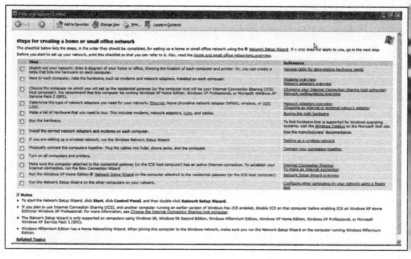

Figure 6-13 Use the checklist to prepare for the imminent network configuration

3. The next screen (shown in Figure 6-14) shows all current network connections that are disconnected from an active network. If you intend any of these connections to be used in the network, you should follow the onscreen advice and plug in the appropriate cable or switch on your Wireless card. If you don't want to use any of the connection media listed in the box, tick the "Ignore disconnected network hardware" checkbox then click on the "Next" button.

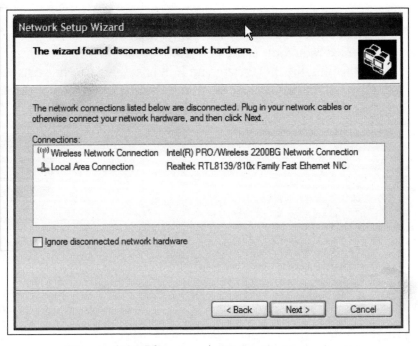

*Figure 6-14 Plug in any connections you want
configured for use on your network*

Some wireless network cards (especially on laptop/notebook computers) are built into the chassis of the PC. Most of these have an external button on the chassis for activating the wireless card. If you see your wireless card is disconnected, try pressing the activation button.

4. The next screen (Figure 6-15) asks you to select the method your PC will use to connect to the rest of the

network. If the machine you are setting up is the Internet
Connection Sharing (ICS) Host, you should select the
topmost radio button then click on "Next". If you are
connecting this PC through an ICS host that already exists
on your network, select the middle radio button then click
"Next".

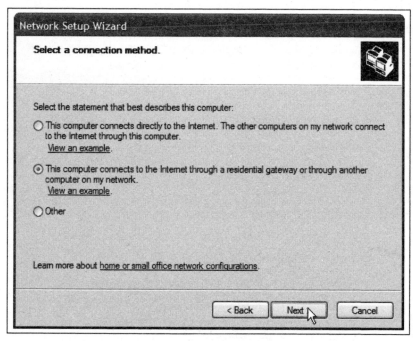

*Figure 6-15 Select the most appropriate method
of connecting your computer to the rest of the
network*

You can click on the "home or small office
network configurations" link to obtain some
more information on how to set up your
network (screen shown in Figure 6-16).

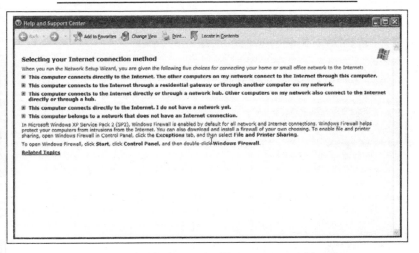

*Figure 6-16 Clicking on "home or small office
network configurations" will launch the Help
and Support Center on networking*

You now have two separate paths you can take through
this procedure: one for the ICS Host computer and the other
for a PC connecting through an ICS Host.

We will cover other connection methods
(obtained through the "Other" radio button on
the screen shown in Figure 6-15) at the end of
this section.

Setting up an ICS Host

To set up an ICS Host computer (the one that all other computers will access the Internet through), you should perform the following steps, using the Network Setup Wizard.

1. When you reach the screen shown in Figure 6-17, select the topmost option then click on "Next".

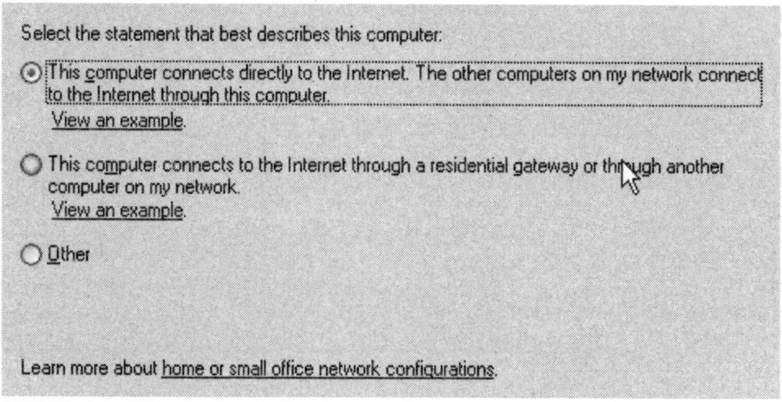

Figure 6-17 Select the topmost radio button to set up an ICS Host

2. On the following screen, shown in Figure 6-18 entitled "Select your Internet connection", you should select the network card or interface being used to connect to your ISP. When you have selected this interface from the list, click on "Next".

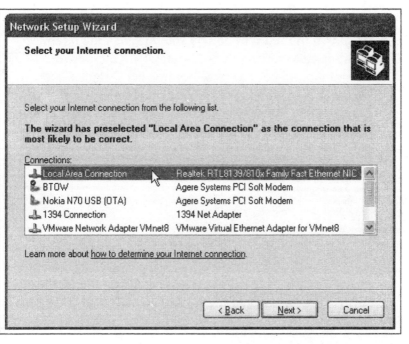

Figure 6-18 Select your internal network interface that computers on your LAN will reference as their default gateway

The interface shown in Figure 6-18 is the "Local Area Connection". This was selected automatically as the most likely interface for using as the ISP interface. However, you can select a different interface if you desire. Simply scroll down the list and highlight your preference before pressing "Next".

3. When you see the "Select your private connection" screen, as shown in Figure 6-19, you should select the interface being used to route other computers on your network to the Internet interface. This will become the Default Gateway for all PCs on your network. Select the interface that is connected to the private side of your network then click on "Next".

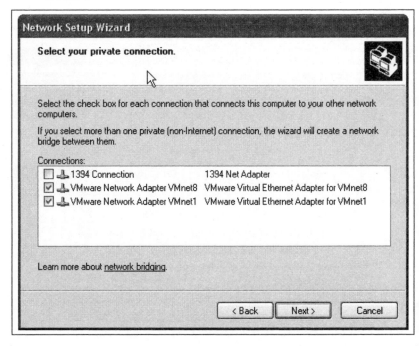

Figure 6-19 Select the private network interface that connects to your LAN

You can call up extra information from the Help and Support Center on network bridging by clicking Network Bridging, see Figure 6-20.

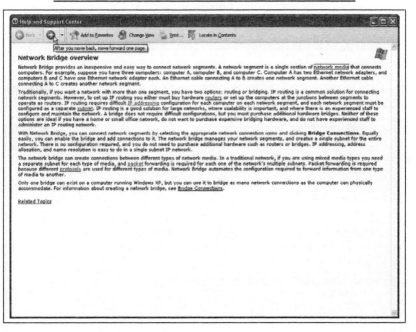

Figure 6-20 Find out more information on Network Bridging from the Help and Support Center

4. On the next screen (shown in Figure 6-21) you have the option of typing in a description of your computer in plain English so that other PC users can easily identify it as the ICS Host system, for example, you could add "ICS Host" as the computer description. If your ISP has asked that you

use a specific computer name for your ICS Host, type the new name of your PC in the "Computer name" text entry field. When you have entered your PC's description and checked the computer name, click "Next".

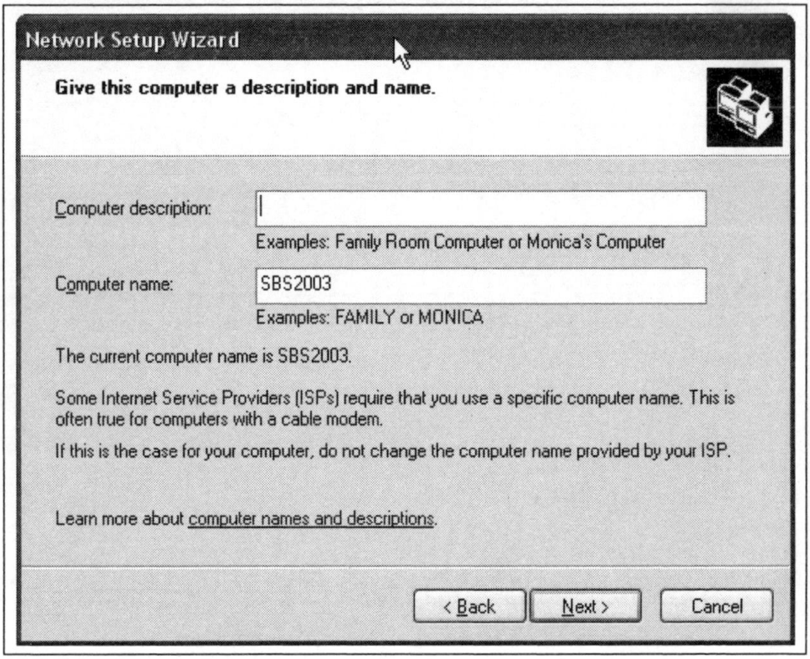

Figure 6-21 Add a meaningful computer description and check the computer name with your ISP if necessary

5. On the "Name your network" screen, type the name of the network as you would like it presented to other users and computers. Some people prefer the home address or office name, while others prefer something related to the network

itself, such as "Wireless" or "HomeLAN". When you have entered the name of your network in the text entry field shown in Figure 6-22, click "Next".

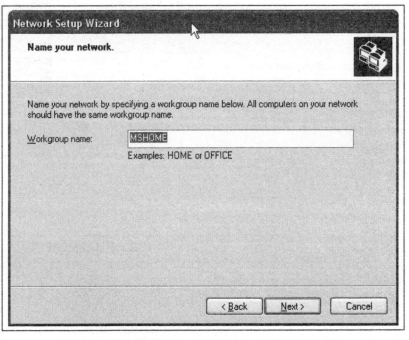

Figure 6-22 Give your network a meaningful name

6. On the "File and printer sharing" page, you can turn on file and print sharing if this is a network feature you want to use, see Figure 6-23. When you have selected your preference, click "Next".

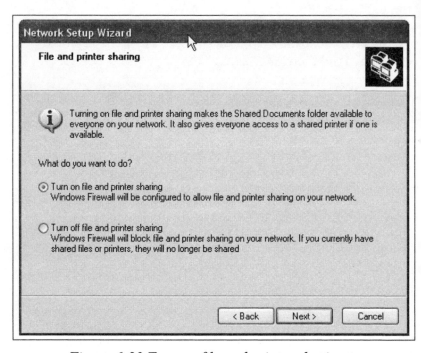

Figure 6-23 Turn on file and printer sharing to share resources on your PC with other network users

If you opt to use "File and printer sharing", a folder called "Shared Documents" will be made available on the network to all users of your workgroup (the computer name you selected in the previous screen). Make sure you do not store sensitive documents in this folder as they will be accessible to all network users.

7. Finally, on the last screen in this wizard (shown in Figure 6-24) you can review your selected configuration then click "Next" to have the wizard apply the configuration changes as necessary.

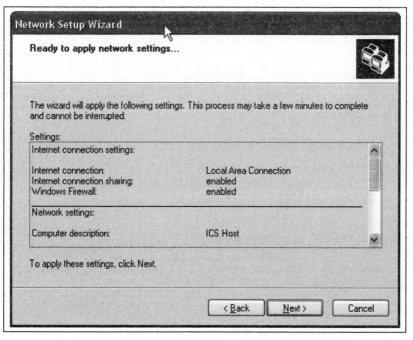

Figure 6-24 Review your configuration before committing it with the "Next" button

You have now successfully set up an ICS host computer and shared resources with other PCs on the network.

Each machine that you would like to connect to the network must also run the Network Setup Wizard and in each case, follow the procedure shown in the next section.

Normal PCs and the Network Setup Wizard

When you have completed the section on setting up an ICS Host computer, each PC you want to use the ICS Host must have the Network Setup Wizard run on it.

The following procedure should be followed for each of these computers:

1. When you see the "Select a connection method" screen (shown in Figure 6-25), select "This computer connects to the Internet through a residential gateway or through another computer on my network" then click "Next".

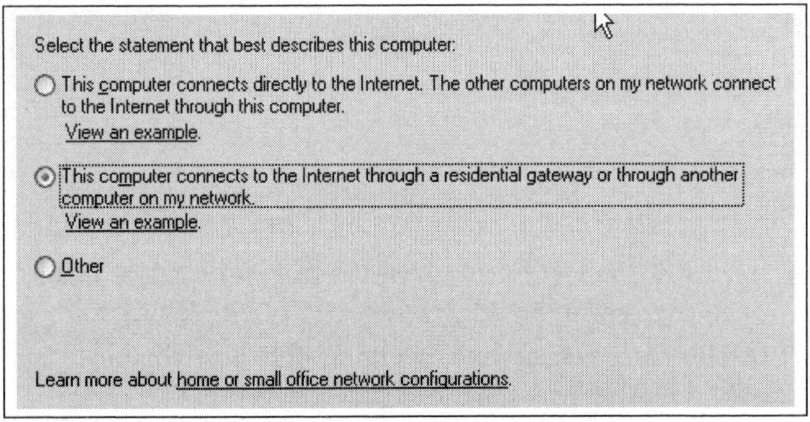

Select the statement that best describes this computer:

○ This computer connects directly to the Internet. The other computers on my network connect to the Internet through this computer.
View an example.

◉ This computer connects to the Internet through a residential gateway or through another computer on my network.
View an example.

○ Other

Learn more about home or small office network configurations.

Figure 6-25 Select this option for all PCs on the network that are NOT the ICS Host

You can click the link "View an example" to see an example of what the physical LAN might be laid out like in the home, see Figure 6-26.

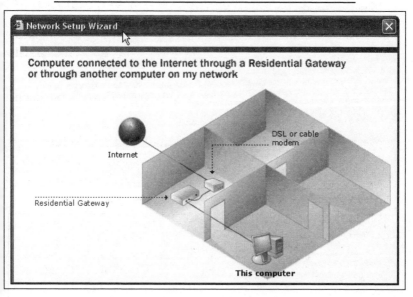

Figure 6-26 This is how the home network might look in a typical LAN environment

2. On the following screen, "Give this computer a description and name", you should type in a meaningful description for the PC you are setting up, for example, "Tony's PC", and if you want to, you can also change the computer name to adhere to any new convention you might have come up with when you were planning your network. Type the text

into the text entry fields, as shown in Figure 6-27 then click the "Next" button when you are done.

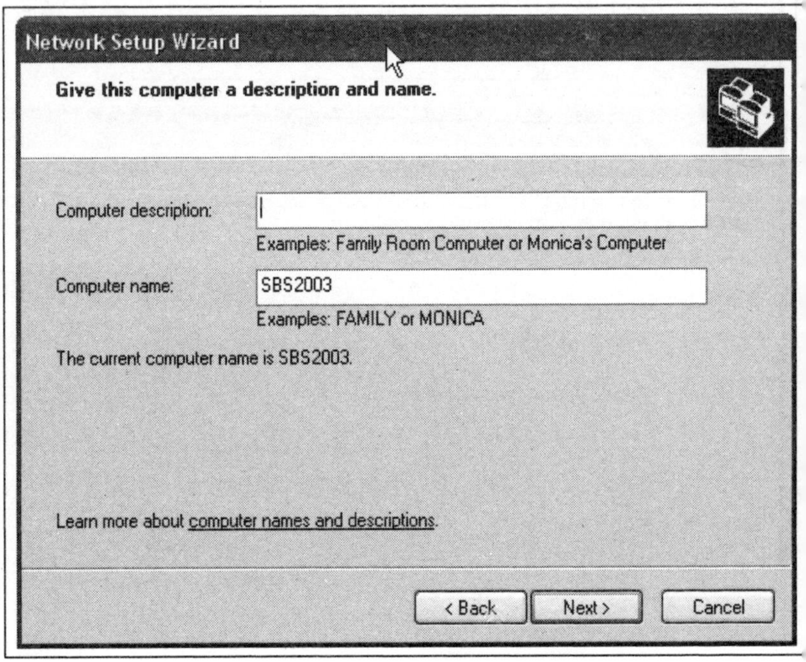

Figure 6-27 Type in a computer description and change the name to adhere to your LAN standards

3. You are now asked to type in the Windows Workgroup name your network has been assigned. This should be the same name you used when you created the ICS Host computer. Type the name into the text entry field shown in Figure 6-28 then click "Next" to continue.

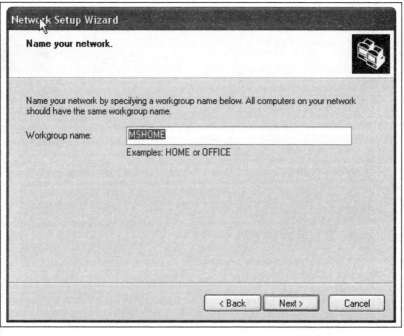

Figure 6-28 Make sure the workgroup name is consistent across all PCs on your network

4. If you want to turn on file and print sharing for this PC on the network, when you see the "File and printer sharing" page, as shown in Figure 6-29, you should select the radio button next to the text, "Turn on file and printer sharing". If you do not want to create the "Shared Documents" folder on this computer, you should select the lower radio button, "Turn off file and printer sharing". When you have made your selection, click on the "Next" button.

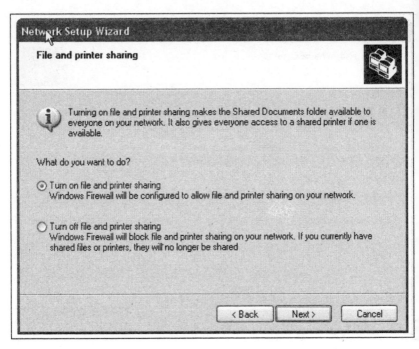

Figure 6-29 Select whether or not to use file and printer sharing on this PC then click Next

5. Finally, on the summary page (shown in Figure 6-30) you should review all the configuration information you entered. When you are content it all looks as intended, you should click "Next".

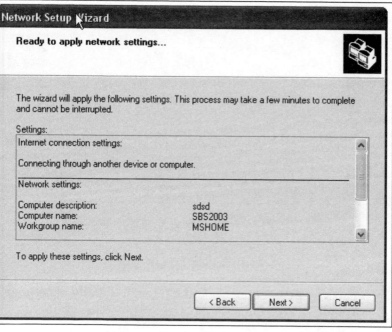

Figure 6-30 Review your network configuration
before pressing the "Next" button

Other Connection Methods

On the "Select a connection method" screen, shown in Figure 6-31, you can select "Other" as the final option not yet explored in this walk-through. Click on the "Next" button to reveal a further three options on how you can configure your PC's networking.

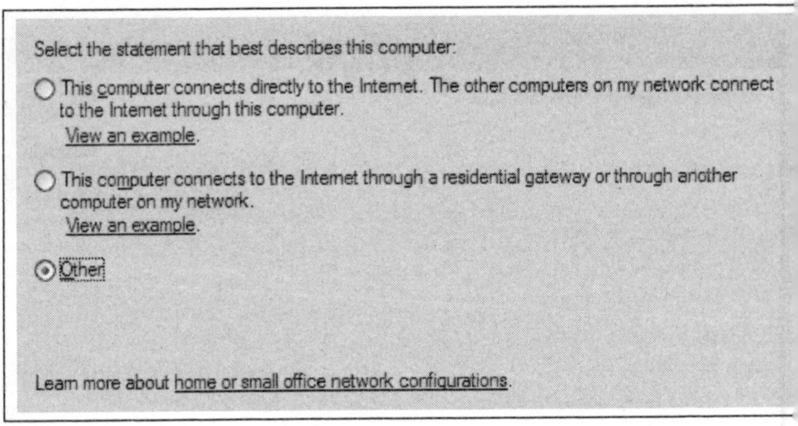

Select the statement that best describes this computer:

○ This computer connects directly to the Internet. The other computers on my network connect to the Internet through this computer.
   View an example.

○ This computer connects to the Internet through a residential gateway or through another computer on my network.
   View an example.

◉ Other

Learn more about home or small office network configurations.

Figure 6-31 Select other to use alternative connection methods

The list of options available are as follows:

- This computer connects to the Internet directly or through a network hub. Other computers on my network also connect to the Internet directly or through a hub.

- This computer connects directly to the Internet. I do not have a network yet.

- This computer belongs to a network that does not have an Internet connection.

Figure 6-32 shows these options.

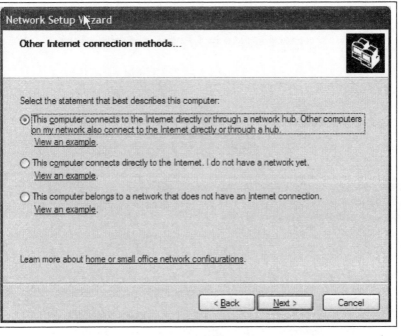

Figure 6-32 Select one of the three alternative connection methods for this computer

If you select the topmost of these options (see the example shown in Figure 6-33 showing three computers connected to the Internet through a hub) your computer is more than likely connecting to the Internet directly through a discrete gateway device (such as a cable modem).

If this is the case, select this option and click "Next".

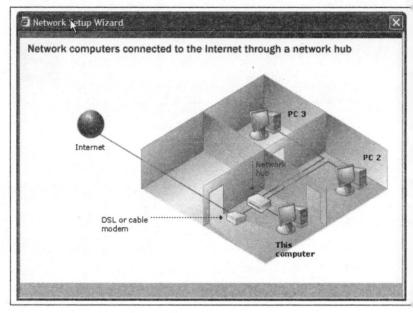

Figure 6-33 This diagram shows the PCs
connected to the Internet through a communal
hub or switch

If you select the middle of the two options, you are telling
Windows XP you do not have a network to connect to but you
are still connecting this PC to the Internet, see Figure 6-34.

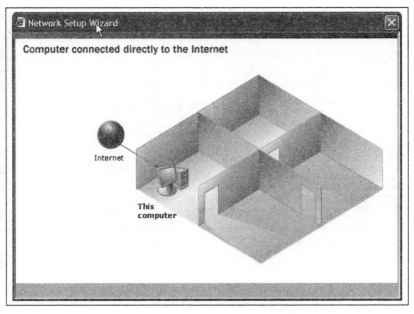

*Figure 6-34 This option is for a single PC
connecting directly to the Internet without
having a LAN to connect to*

Finally, the bottom option in the list is for computers that exist
on a LAN but do not route to the Internet in any way. In this
case, there will be no default gateway defined on the system
since there is no external Internet connection to route to, see
Figure 6-35.

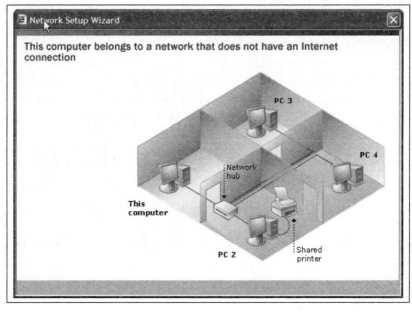

Figure 6-35 This option is for LANs with no external Internet connection

In each case, when you have selected the option that applies to your LAN and Internet configuration, select the appropriate radio button from the list then click on "Next".

You should then follow the wizard through the steps already covered, typing in the computer name, computer description and Windows Workgroup information when asked.

Firewall Configuration

The Service Pack 2 (SP2) update for Windows XP Home and Windows XP Professional introduced a new, improved Windows Firewall, integrated into a central control facility called the Windows Security Center (shown in Figure 6-36).

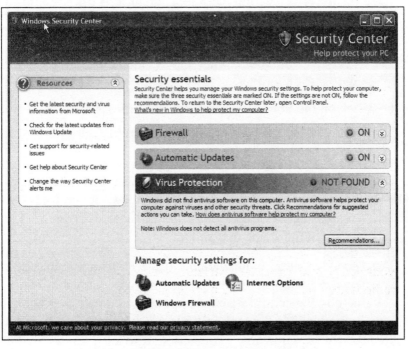

Figure 6-36 The Windows Security Center is a central control facility for the Firewall, Automatic Updates and Anti-virus software

You can use the Windows Security Center to view the status of the Windows Firewall on your PC, as well as getting an idea of how your PC uses Automatic Updates (from the Windows Update Internet site) and how well your virus protection is configured.

This brief section will look at turning the Windows Firewall on and off for specific connections, using the interface provided through the Windows Security Center.

Firstly, you should start the Windows Security Center by doing the following:

1. Click on the Start Menu then select Control Panel
2. When you see the Control Panel, shown in Figure 6-37, click on Security Center.

> The Security Center is available in both the Category view and the Classic view. In both cases the Security Center is represented by an icon in the shape of a shield.

The Security Center is unavailable if the PC is a member of a Windows domain. In his case, the security of each PC is governed by the central management of the domain and not by each individual PC. To look at Windows Firewall details in the context of a domain, you should open up Network Connections (again from the Control Panel), right-click the connection you are interested in, click Properties then select Advanced. If you click Setting, you will be able to configure the Windows Firewall from here.

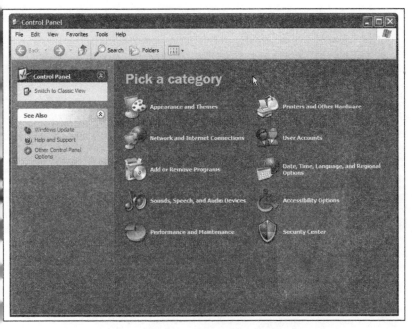

*Figure 6-37 Click on Security Center to launch
the Windows Security Center*

3. When the Windows Security Center starts up, you will see
the current operational status of your Windows Firewall on
your PC, see Figure 6-38. The status can be either "On" or
"Off", as shown in Figure 6-39. This binary toggle can be
used to quickly switch off the Windows Firewall if you are
experiencing connectivity problems and suspect your
Windows Firewall is blocking your external connection.

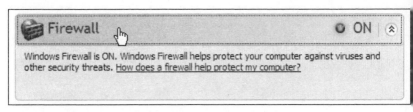

Figure 6-38 Check the operational status of the Windows Firewall. In this case it is set to ON

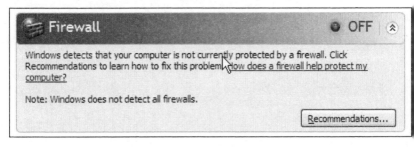

Figure 6-39 In this Figure you can see the Windows Firewall status is OFF

4. If the Windows Firewall is OFF, you can click on Recommendations... to be offered some remedial action as to how to turn it back on again, see Figure 6-40.

If your Windows Firewall is OFF, you are open to attack from hackers or Internet worms unless you have alternative means of protection. Unless absolutely necessary, the Windows Firewall should remain switched on at all times.

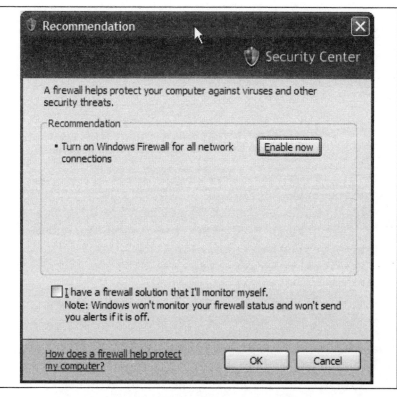

*Figure 6-40 Click "Enable now" to switch the
Windows Firewall back on again*

5. If you do not need the Windows Firewall, you can click on
the checkbox "I have a firewall solution that I'll monitor
myself". If you do this and click OK, you will see the
status of the Windows Firewall in the Windows Security
Center change to say that the Windows Firewall is "NOT
MONITORED", see Figure 6-41.

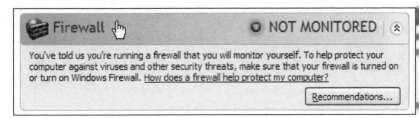

*Figure 6-41 The Firewall is switched off and
you have instructed Windows XP you are using
another product*

6. If your Windows Firewall is switched off and you would
    like to reactivate it, click "Enable now" on the screen
    shown in Figure 6-40. If this is successful, you will see the
    message shown in Figure 6-42. Click "Close" to return to
    the Windows Security Center.

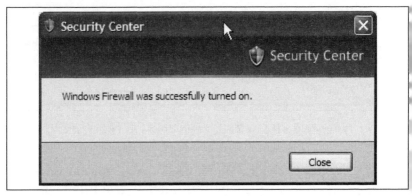

Figure 6-42 The Firewall is activated

7. At the bottom of the Windows Security Center (shown in
    Figure 6-43) you will see the "Manage security settings
    for:" task panel. Click on Windows Firewall.

Manage security settings for:

 Automatic Updates **Internet Options**

 Windows Firewall

*Figure 6-43 Click Windows Firewall to
configure firewall settings*

8. The following dialog box immediately starts on the
Windows Firewall General properties tab (as shown in
Figure 6-44). This dialog box gives you the option of
switching the Windows Firewall on or off, as well as
selecting a checkbox that stops Windows Firewall
exceptions from being processed. As security is covered in
more detail later in this book, for now we will concentrate
of making sure the Windows Firewall is working and
guarding the connections you require it to police. Select
the Advanced tab at the top of the screen.

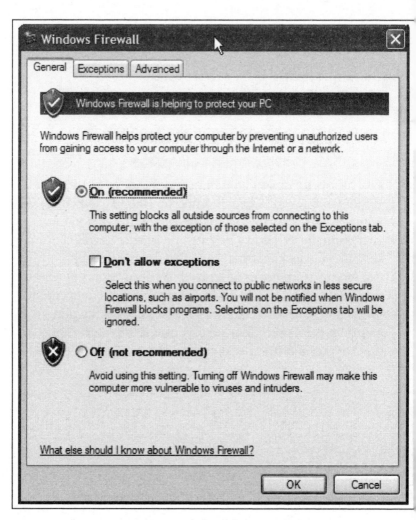

*Figure 6-44 Select the Advanced tab to see how
the Windows Firewall has been activated on
specific network connections*

9. The Advanced screen (shown in Figure 6-45) shows a list of network connections, each of which has a checkbox next to it. If you want a specific connection to have the Firewall either activated or deactivated, place a tick in the checkbox accordingly.

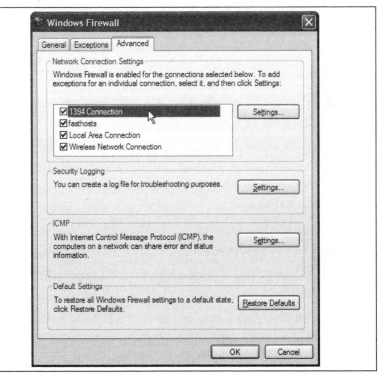

Figure 6-45 Check the checkbox next to each network connection you want to protect

Ok, that's all we'll cover at this stage on security. Next, we will look at the detailed properties of a network connection.

Network Connection Properties

Each network connection has the potential to operate in a completely different way. Some are dial-up connections, with their own specific requirements for using a modem to connect to an ISP for example, others might be VPNs for securely connecting a computer to a remote network over a 'bearer' network that is inherently insecure, such as the Internet. Whatever the requirement, the interface for configuring your network connection remains consistent, with additional capability and configuration for that interface presented in the standard interface where appropriate.

All of your network connections are available in the Network Connections window, available through the Control Panel. To access the Network Connection window, you should do the following:

1. Click on the Start menu
2. Click on Control Panel
3. In the Control Panel click on Network and Internet Connections
4. Click on Network Connections in the bottom half of the screen. This will open the Network Connections windows, as shown in Figure 6-46.

Figure 6-46 The Network Connections windows

Each of the network connection icons shown in the main window on the right-hand side of the screen contains information about the status of that connection.

If you click on any one connection, further information for that connection is displayed on the left-hand side of the screen under "Details".

This information is as follows:

- The connection name

- The connection type, for example: dial-up

- Its current connection status, for example: connected, firewalled

- The hardware device

- The MAC address of the NIC
- The IP address, subnet mask and how the IP addressing information was assigned, i.e. was it assigned manually or through a DHCP server.

The information contained in this "Details" pane, is extracted from the connection's properties. To look at any specific connection's properties, right-click on the connection icon in the Network Connections windows and select properties. This will launch the dialog box shown in Figure 6-47.

Figure 6-47 Network Connection properties

The General tab (Figure 6-47) of the network connection properties gives you top-level configuration information about the connection and the hardware it's using, such as in the case shown in the Figure where the dial-up connection shown is using the inbuilt modem (AC97 Soft Data Fax Modem with SmartCP), connected to COM3 (communications port 3) and it lists the telephone number this dial-up connection uses to contact the ISP.

At the bottom of this General tab, you can tick the checkbox, "Show icon in notification area when connected" (see Figure 6-48) if you want a small networking icon to appear in the bottom right-hand corner of the task bar, as shown in Figure 6-49.

Figure 6-48 Select this option to display an icon in the system tray

Figure 6-49 The network connection icon is two overlapping PCs

If you click on the "ConFigure" button just beneath the connection interface (in this case the modem) you are taken to a new dialog box that can be used to change the characteristics of that hardware device, see Figure 6-50.

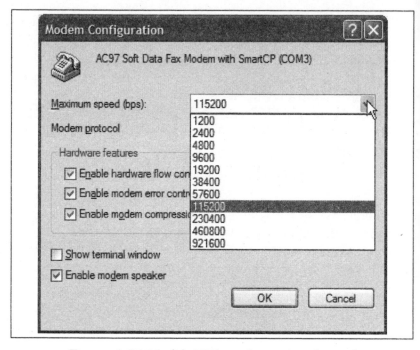

Figure 6-50 Modify NIC configuration through this interface

In this example, you can change the maximum connection speed the modem can communicate at (a modem automatically connects at the fastest speed it can, however there may be times, under the guidance of an ISP, where you might want a lower maximum speed). Other hardware features affecting the way the modem communicates are changed here. Your ISP will advise you if you need to change the settings beneath the "Hardware features" heading on this page.

If you do not want to hear the modem dialling and synchronising the connecting with the ISP, you can uncheck this checkbox. However, when diagnosing a fault, it is sometimes useful to listen to this initial handshaking to see when a signal may drop.

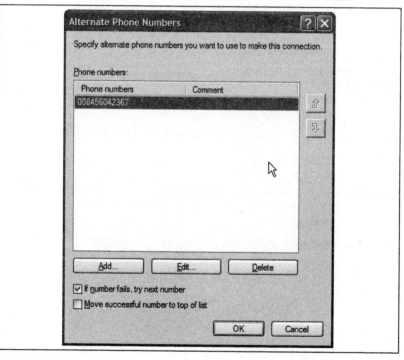

Figure 6-51 Use dialling alternates to progressively dial a list of ISP numbers

If you click on the "Alternates" button, as shown in Figure 6-51, on the "General" screen, you can add or remove alternative numbers that are used to contact your ISP.

In this way you can configure Windows XP to automatically dial a list of numbers, each time trying the next in the list if the last number fails (for example, if the number is engaged).

If you reveal the properties of a LAN connection, rather than the previous example of a dial-up connection, a slightly different collection of information is displayed, see Figure 6-52.

On this screen, you will see the network interface device shown at the top of the screen, a variety of connection specific configuration details in the middle section of the dialog box, immediately followed by a description of the service that is currently highlighted in the list, finished off with two checkboxes that allow you to display a connection network connection icon in the system tray, and the option to send notifications if there is limited connectivity.

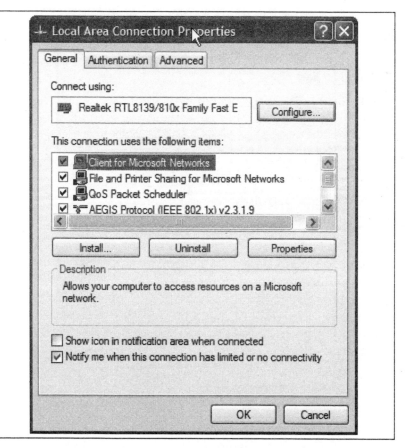

Figure 6-52 The LAN NIC properties page

If you click on "ConFigure" (next to the hardware device at the top of the screen) the Windows Device Manager properties dialog box for that hardware device will be launched, see Figure 6-53.

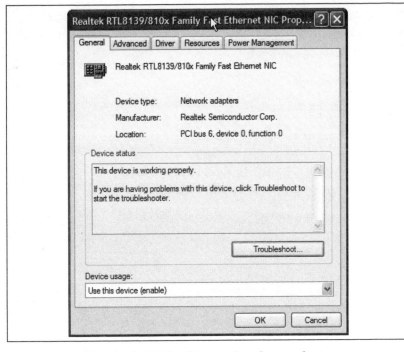

Figure 6-53 ConFigure hardware device characteristics using the Windows Device manager Properties dialog box

If you are having problems with your LAN card not working as you would expect, you can click on the "Troubleshoot…" button to run through a set of questions looking to determine a resolution.

Concentrating on the item list in the middle of the screen, as shown in Figure 6-54, you can adjust the configuration and connection details for a specific connection regarding Microsoft Networking, file and printer sharing, and your TCP/IP configuration.

Figure 6-54 This list shows the configuration items for use by this connection

If you highlight any one of the items shown in the list (as shown in Figure 6-54) you can click the "Properties" button immediately beneath the list to reveal individual list items for that configuration information. The one we are going to elaborate on is the TCP/IP configuration item, see Figure 6-55.

You might have to scroll down the list to find the Internet Protocol (TCP/IP) list item.

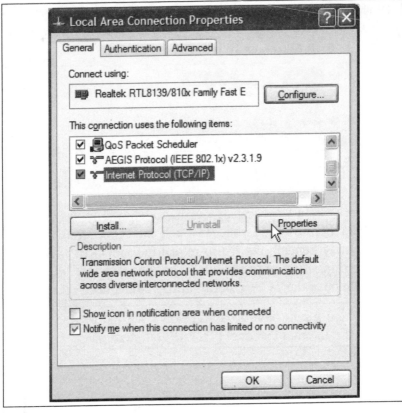

Figure 6-55 Click on Properties to review TCP/IP settings

TCP/IP Properties

From the interface, shown in Figure 6-56, you will configure everything related to TCP/IP.

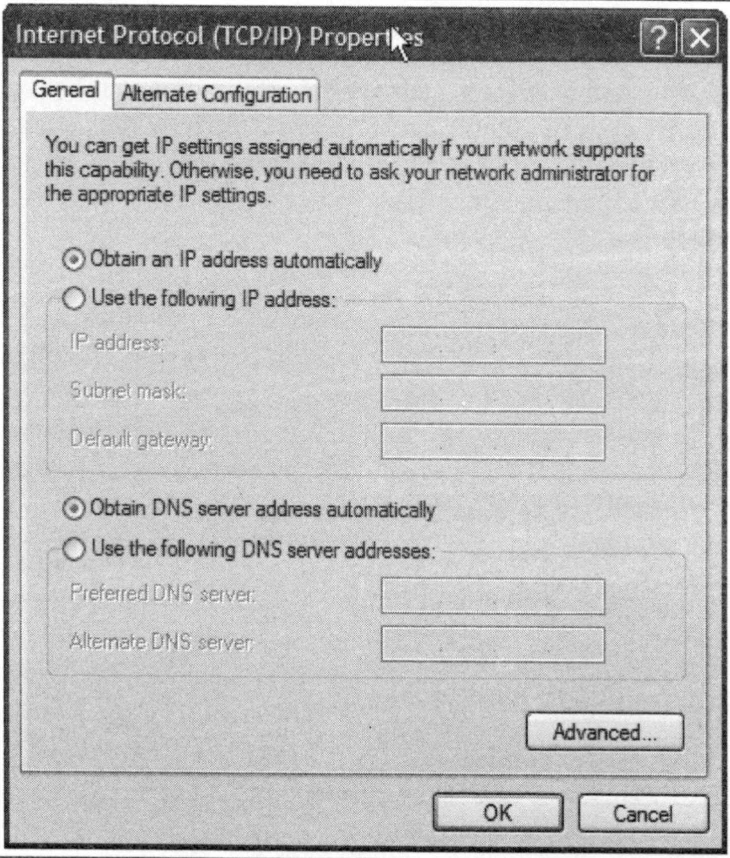

*Figure 6-56 All aspects of TCP/IP
configuration is carried out using this interface*

Starting at the top of the dialog box shown in Figure 6-56, if the radio button next to "Obtain an IP address automatically" is selected, your network interface will obtain its TCP/IP addressing information from a DHCP server. If this is the case, you can use the IPCONFIG command from the Windows Command Line to see the addressing information that has been allocated from the server, see Figure 6-57. To do this, click on Start > Run then type cmd.exe and press Return. When you see the command line, type IPCONFIG /ALL and press Return.

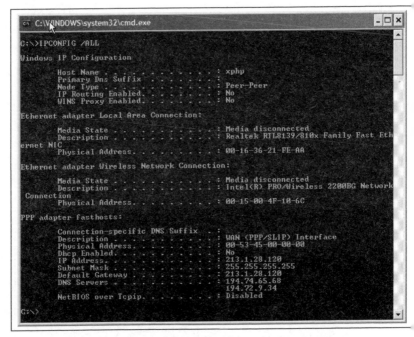

Figure 6-57 IPCONFIG /ALL shows all TCP/IP addressing information for all networking adapters on your system

If you are not using DHCP to receive your addressing information (some ISPs prefer you to use specific IP address details) you will see a screen looking something like that shown in Figure 6-58.

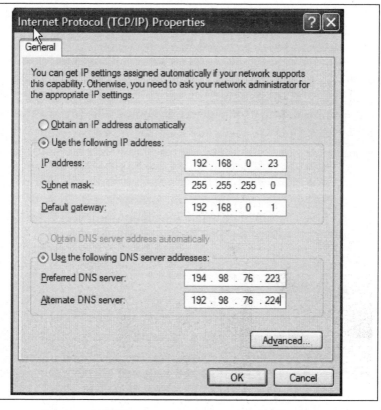

Figure 6-58 If you are not using DHCP you will see specific TCP/IP address details for this connection

Your ICS host computer will act as a DHCP server for all other computers on your LAN. It will manage a DHCP set of addresses that are private to your LAN, and route these to the Internet through a system called Network Address Translation (NAT).

If you have used the Network Setup Wizard to configure your network, it will be unlikely you will need to change any of your TCP/IP configuration information. However, when you are troubleshooting your network connection (if you run into problems) then it pays dividends to know where these configuration selections are held and how they are managed.

All network interfaces can have the TCP/IP properties configured in this way. You will need to navigate each interface until you find the item list, but rest assured it will be there.

Summary

It is highly recommended that you use the Network Setup Wizard to set up your home or small business network. The wizard will be able to make all the modifications to the systems on your LAN that are required to get your systems communicating, and it will ensure that you don't need to become a networking guru to set up a simple system in your home.

However, it's a good idea to dig around a little in case you do run into problems and in many of the interfaces you've looked at, there is a fairly good help facility that can elaborate on any of the individual steps.

If you follow the guidelines in this chapter, you will have a network. It's as easy as that. The rest of this book looks at ways of making use of your network, how to secure your network and in the unlikely event of something going wrong, how to troubleshoot your network.

PART 4
Troubleshooting

7

Troubleshooting Connectivity

Ok, let's be honest, no matter how well you have set up and configured your network, eventually things go wrong. It's happened to us all, and it's certainly nothing to worry about.

This chapter will give you some insight into a few of the built-in tools that you can use to help troubleshoot some connectivity problems. These are not the only tools available, but they are the best first step.

Firstly, you should check everything is powered up correctly and is plugged in where it should be. More often than not, it can be the simplest of things that causes the problem and you don't want to spend hours troubleshooting a problem only to find the power cable on the wireless access point was accidentally pulled out.

Table 7-1 shows a simple checklist of things you should check first.

Check	Action
is the power switched on to all the devices?	Check the power and try again.
are all the cables and connectors plugged in?	Remove cables and plug them back in again.
can you see flashing or blinking lights on the devices?	This can indicate network activity – if they are not flashing, this could be where the problem resides.
have you added any new kit?	If so, what was it and can you remove it and try again?
have you installed any new software or hardware drivers?	If so, what was it and can you remove it and try again?

Table 7-1 This table shows a basic checklist of possible problem areas that should be checked first

Tools of the Trade

We are going to examine some of the built-in Windows XP tools that can be used to troubleshoot connectivity problems.

For each of the tools we will look at the syntax and parameters, and in each case explain what they are used for. We will also provide a simple example to demonstrate usage.

Unless otherwise stated, all the tools must be run from the a command prompt. To get to the command prompt, click on Start then select Run. Type CMD in the dialogue entry box then press Return.

By the end of this chapter you will have a much better idea of what each tool does and how it could be of help to you in troubleshooting your own network environment.

Some tools are easy to use, others however can be quite complicated. It is worth doing some further reading on each if you are not sure how or when to use them.

IPCONFIG

This tool displays the TCP/IP network configuration information of your computer and can be used to refresh DHCP and DNS settings.

If the tool is used without any parameters being specified, it displays the IP address, subnet mask and the default gateway for any installed network adaptors.

Figure 7-1 The output from ipconfig, at first glance, looks daunting until you look at the detail

Syntax

ipconfig [/**all**] [/**renew** [*adapter*]] [/**release** [*adapter*]] [/**flushdns**] [/**displaydns**] [/**registerdns**] [/**showclassid** *adapter*] [/**setclassid** *adapter* [*ClassID*]]

Parameters

/**all** : This parameter displays the full TCP/IP configuration for all adaptors. Adapters can be physical interfaces, such as network cards, or logical interfaces, such as dial-up connections.

/**renew** [*adapter*] : This parameter renews the DHCP configuration for all adapters. You can specify an adapter by using the *adapter* parameter and using the adapter name. You can only use this parameter if the adapter is set up to use DHCP.

/**release** [*adapter*] : This parameter is used to discard the current DHCP configuration for all adaptors or for a specific adapter if using the *adapter* parameter.

/**flushdns** : This parameter is used to flush and then reset the DNS client resolver cache. This can also be used to remove entries that have been added to DNS dynamically.

/**displaydns** : This parameter is used to display the contents of the DNS client resolver cache.

/**registerdns** : This parameter is used to initiate a manual dynamic registration for the DNS names and IP addresses that are configured at a computer. The DNS settings in the advanced properties of the TCP/IP protocol determine which names are registered in DNS.

/showclassid *adapter* : This parameter displays the DHCP class ID for a specific adaptor. In order to display the IDs for all adaptors, use the asterisk (*) wildcard in place of *adapter*.

/setclassid adapter [*ClassID*] : This parameter is used to configure the DHCP class ID for a specific adaptor. In order to set the ID's for all adaptors, use the asterisk (*) wildcard in place of *adapter*.

/? : This parameter displays help (as shown in Figure 7-1)

ipconfig is the tool within Windows XP that replaced winipcfg from Windows 95, Millennium and 98.

It would be useful to keep a copy in a file of your ipconfig information, in case you need it at a later stage. You can do this from a DOS prompt by typing *ipconfig /all >c:\ipconfig.txt*

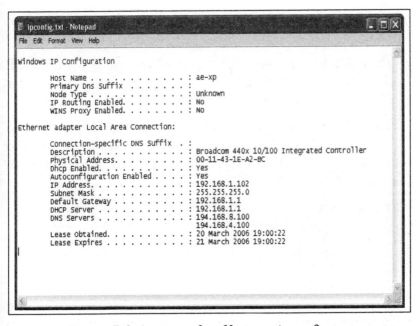

```
ipconfig.txt - Notepad
File  Edit  Format  View  Help

Windows IP Configuration

        Host Name . . . . . . . . . . . . : ae-xp
        Primary DNS Suffix  . . . . . . . :
        Node Type . . . . . . . . . . . . : Unknown
        IP Routing Enabled. . . . . . . . : No
        WINS Proxy Enabled. . . . . . . . : No

Ethernet adapter Local Area Connection:

        Connection-specific DNS Suffix  . :
        Description . . . . . . . . . . . : Broadcom 440x 10/100 Integrated Controller
        Physical Address. . . . . . . . . : 00-11-43-1E-A2-BC
        Dhcp Enabled. . . . . . . . . . . : Yes
        Autoconfiguration Enabled . . . . : Yes
        IP Address. . . . . . . . . . . . : 192.168.1.102
        Subnet Mask . . . . . . . . . . . : 255.255.255.0
        Default Gateway . . . . . . . . . : 192.168.1.1
        DHCP Server . . . . . . . . . . . : 192.168.1.1
        DNS Servers . . . . . . . . . . . : 194.168.8.100
                                            194.168.4.100
        Lease Obtained. . . . . . . . . . : 20 March 2006 19:00:22
        Lease Expires . . . . . . . . . . : 21 March 2006 19:00:22
```

Figure 7-2 An example of how an ipconfig text file might look

You can also find out some of the same information in Windows via a graphical view by viewing network connections and right-clicking on the adaptor you are interested in and selecting the Support tab (as shown in Figure 7-3).

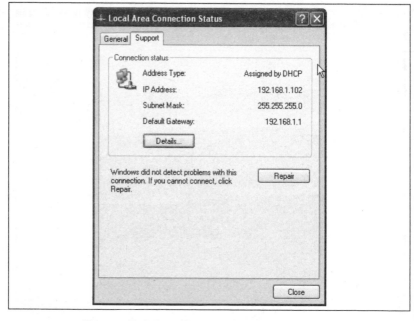

Figure 7-3 Local Area Connection Status
Support tab

PING

Ping is a tool that is used to verify IP connectivity to another computer by sending ICMP Echo Request messages.

You can use ping to test both the IP address and computer name you are trying to contact.

If you can ping the IP address but not the computer name then there might be a name resolution issue.

This is the best tool to use to troubleshoot connectivity and should probably be your first step!

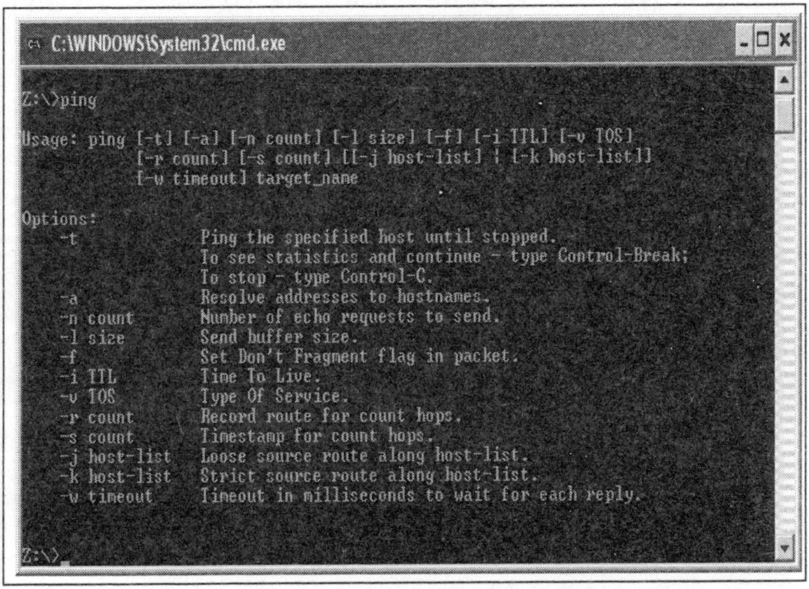

Figure 7-4 Typing Ping without qualifiers or switches will display the syntax

Syntax

ping [-t] [-a] [-n *count*] [-l *size*] [-f] [-i *TTL*] [-v *TOS*] [-r *count*] [-s *count*] [-j *host-list*] [-k *host-list*] [-w *timeout*] [*target_name*]

Parameters

-t : This parameter specifies that ping continues sending messages to the destination address until it is stopped. To stop and display statistics press CTRL-BREAK, to stop and quit press CTRL-C.

-a : This parameter is used to display the reverse name resolution on the destination IP address to show the host name.

-n *count* : This parameter is used to specify the number of Echo request messages sent. The default number is 4.

-l *size* : This parameter is used to specify the Data field length in bytes in the Echo request messages. The default size is 32 and the maximum size is 65,527.

-f : This parameter is used to specify that the Echo request messages are sent with the "Don't Fragment" flag in the IP header set to a value of 1.

-i *TTL* : This parameter is used to specify the value in the TTL field in the IP header. The default is the default TTL value for the host. For Windows XP hosts, the value is typically 128 and the maximum is 255.

-v *TOS* : This parameter is used to specify the value for the Type of Service (TOS) field in the IP header. The default is 0 and the maximum is 255.

-r *count* : This parameter is used to specify that the Record Route option in the IP header is used to record the path taken by the Echo request message and reply message. Each hop in the path adds an entry. The *count* must be a minimum of 1 and a maximum of 9.

-s *count* : This parameter is used to specify that the Internet Timestamp option in the IP header is used to record the time of arrival for the Echo Request message and reply message for each hop. The *count* must be a minimum of 1 and a maximum of 4.

-j *host-list* : This parameter is used to specify that the Echo Request messages use the Loose Source Route option in the IP header with the set of intermediate destinations specified in *host-list*. With loose source routeing, successive intermediate destinations can be separated by one or more routers. The maximum number of entries in the host-list is 9.

-k *host-list* : This parameter is used to specify that the Echo Request messages use the Strict Source Route option in the IP header with the set of intermediate destinations specified in *host-list*. With strict source routeing, the next intermediate destination must be directly reachable. The maximum number of entries in the host-list is 9.

-w *timeout* : This parameter is used to specify the amount of time, in milliseconds, to wait for a reply to be received.

target_name : This parameter is used to specify the amount of time in milliseconds to wait for either a response or to time-out. The default time-out is 4,000 milliseconds (or 4 seconds).

/? : This parameter displays help (as shown in Figure 7-4)

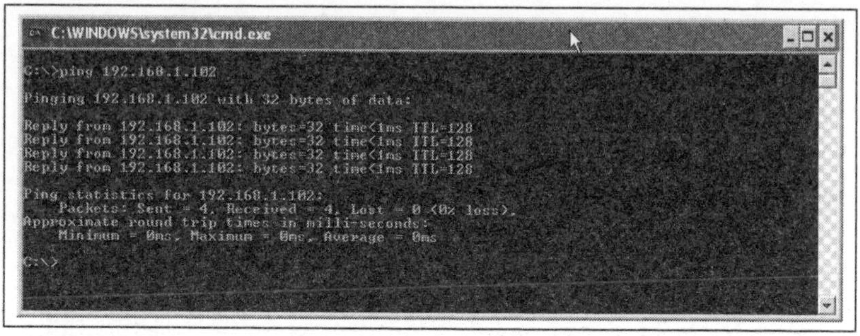

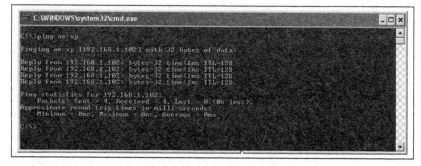

Figure 7-5 An example showing the pinging of an IP address

Figure 7-6 An example showing the pinging of a computer name

Always try to ping the device that is furthest away, and then work backwards. However, make sure you try to ping your own computer and your router as well.

TRACERT

This tool displays the path taken between computers, for example, your computer and another one. It works by sending ICMP Echo Request messages to the destination with increasing Time to Live (TTL) values. The path that is displayed when using the tool is the list of near-side router interfaces in the path between the source and destination. The near-side router interface is the closest one to the sending host used in the path.

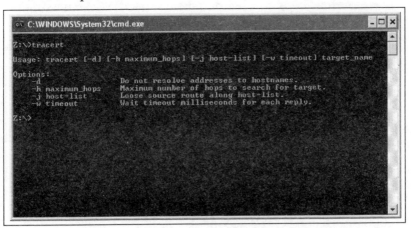

Figure 7-7 An example showing the syntax of the tracert command

Tracert is considered an advanced tool and you might get confusing results.

Syntax

Tracert [**-d**] [**-h** *maximum_hops*] [**-j** *host-list*] [**-w** *timeout*] [*target_name*]

Parameters

-d : This parameter prevents the resolution of IP addresses of intermediate routers to their names. This can increase the speed in which results are displayed.

-h *maximum_hops* : This parameter specifies the maximum number of hops to search for the destination. The default number is 30 hops.

-j *host-list* : This parameter specifies that the messages use the Loose Source Route option in the IP header with the set of intermediate destinations specified in *host-list*. A host-list is a series of IP addresses separated by spaces. The maximum number in the list is 9.

-w *timeout* : This parameter specifies the amount of time in milliseconds to wait for either a response or to time-out. An asterisk (*) is displayed if not received. The default time-out is 4,000 milliseconds (or 4 seconds).

***target_name* :** This parameter specifies the destination either by an IP address or by a host name

-? : This parameter displays help (as shown in Figure 7-7)

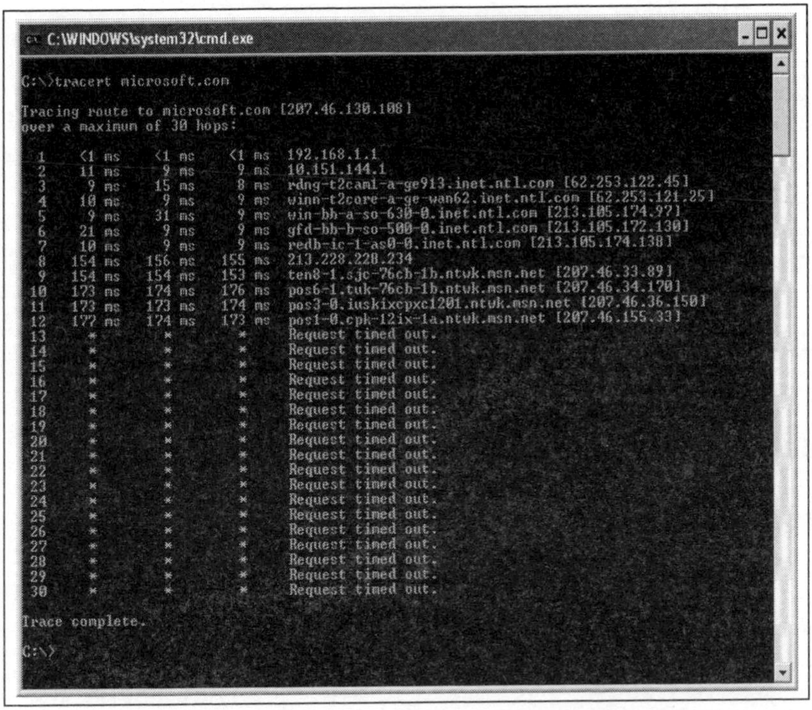

```
C:\WINDOWS\system32\cmd.exe                                        _ □ x

C:\>tracert microsoft.com

Tracing route to microsoft.com [207.46.130.108]
over a maximum of 30 hops:

  1    <1 ms    <1 ms    <1 ms  192.168.1.1
  2    11 ms     9 ms     9 ms  10.151.144.1
  3     9 ms    15 ms     8 ms  rdng-t2cam1-a-ge913.inet.ntl.com [62.253.122.45]
  4    10 ms     9 ms     9 ms  winn-t2core-a-ge-wan62.inet.ntl.com [62.253.121.25]
  5     9 ms    31 ms     9 ms  win-bb-a-so-630-0.inet.ntl.com [213.105.174.97]
  6    21 ms     9 ms     9 ms  gfd-bb-b-so-500-0.inet.ntl.com [213.105.172.130]
  7    10 ms     9 ms     9 ms  redb-ic-1-as0-0.inet.ntl.com [213.105.174.138]
  8   154 ms   156 ms   155 ms  213.228.220.234
  9   154 ms   154 ms   153 ms  ten8-1.sjc-76cb-1b.ntwk.msn.net [207.46.33.89]
 10   173 ms   174 ms   176 ms  pos6-1.tuk-76cb-1b.ntwk.msn.net [207.46.34.170]
 11   173 ms   173 ms   174 ms  pos3-0.iuskixcpxc1201.ntwk.msn.net [207.46.36.150]
 12   177 ms   174 ms   173 ms  pos1-0.cpk-12ix-1a.ntwk.msn.net [207.46.155.33]
 13     *        *        *      Request timed out.
 14     *        *        *      Request timed out.
 15     *        *        *      Request timed out.
 16     *        *        *      Request timed out.
 17     *        *        *      Request timed out.
 18     *        *        *      Request timed out.
 19     *        *        *      Request timed out.
 20     *        *        *      Request timed out.
 21     *        *        *      Request timed out.
 22     *        *        *      Request timed out.
 23     *        *        *      Request timed out.
 24     *        *        *      Request timed out.
 25     *        *        *      Request timed out.
 26     *        *        *      Request timed out.
 27     *        *        *      Request timed out.
 28     *        *        *      Request timed out.
 29     *        *        *      Request timed out.
 30     *        *        *      Request timed out.

Trace complete.

C:\>
```

*Figure 7-8 See how the tracert command offers
feedback on every stage of an IP connection*

Figure 7-8 shows a standard tracert to Microsoft.com. Notice
that after the 12th hop the request times out. This could be for
any number of reasons, most likely that a router or firewall is
blocking the action.

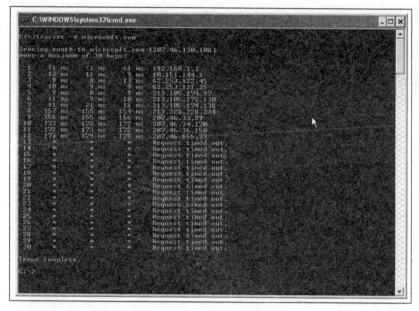

Figure 7-9 Output from the tracert –d switch

Figure 7-9 shows a tracert -d to Microsoft.com. Notice that this time only the IP addresses are displayed.

Help and Support Wizards

If you are using Windows XP, you can always try some of the wizards and help files located in the Help and Support Center, which can be located on the START menu.

Select Networking and the Web from the Pick a Help Topic on the left-hand side of the screen to display the available help.

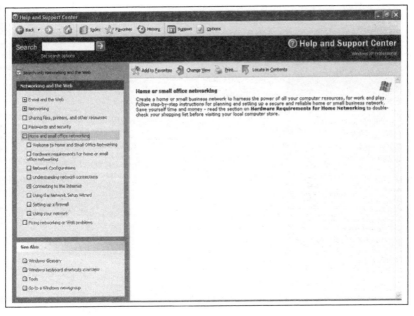

Figure 7-10 Windows XP Help and Support Center

There are many different help topics and wizards you can use here. The best thing to do is to have a look and see if the problem you are having is covered, and if it is, read through the available help and follow any suggested actions.

We are going to walk you through the Fixing a networking problem wizard.

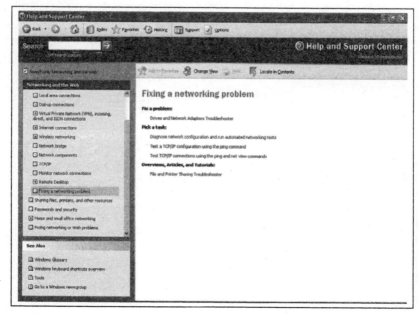

*Figure 7-11 Fixing a networking problem
wizard*

Select the Diagnose network configuration and run automated networking tests from the task list.

This scans your system to obtain information about your hardware, software and network connections.

You can choose to start a scan or to change the scanning options. Make sure that the options selected include the checks you want performed, then select Scan your system. This process should only take a few moments.

As you will be able to see in Figure 7-12, the displayed results contain a lot of potentially useful information, including your IP address and network card details. You will also notice that the tool performs a number of tests, including performing a ping against your computer, the default gateway, etc.

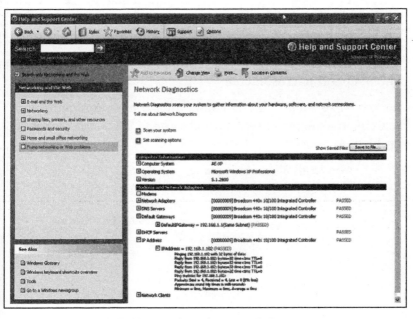

Figure 7-12 Results of Network Diagnostics scan

Summary

If, after trying some of the tools mentioned throughout this chapter, you are still having trouble, there are a number of places you can go to for additional help.

You should always consult the manufacturer of the equipment that is causing you the problem, assuming you know which piece of equipment is the problem.

You can always try the Microsoft Support website at http://support.microsoft.com

Have a look through some of the newsgroups or do a search on Google – someone else may have had a similar problem to you.

Above all else, don't panic.

PART 5
Advanced Networking

8

Advanced Setup

In this section we will be looking at some of the more advanced features such as sharing files, folders and printers, how to use Internet Connection Sharing to share your Internet connection to all your networked computers and how to quickly configure Outlook Express to start sending and receiving email.

> All of the screenshots and explanations in this chapter are based on Windows XP SP2.

File Sharing

Sharing files with others on your network, or even with other users of your computer is a very easy process. This section looks at some of the ways of sharing files such as pictures and even entire folders.

Shared Folders enables multiple users of the same computer to share files with each other no matter who is logged on to the computer at the time. In the same way that each user has a My Documents, My Pictures and My Music set of folders, there are also Shared Documents, Shared Pictures and Shared Music folders, as shown in Figure 8-1.

So, if you want to share your holiday pictures with someone else who uses the computer, or uses another computer on the same network, just copy them to the Shared Pictures directory, and hey presto, they can see them.

To share, just open My Documents, and then click and drag the file or folder that you want to share to the Shared Documents area within Other Places, as shown in Figure 8-2.

Figure 8-1 Shared folders

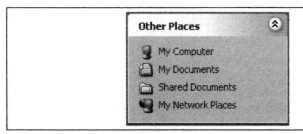

Figure 8-2 Shared documents in other places

The other way to share an entire folder is to right-click the folder, select the Sharing tab and choose whether you want to set up "Local sharing and security", in which case just drag the folder to the Shared Documents folder, although you do have the option of making the folder private so that only you have access or the other option of "Network sharing and security". If you want the network option you just tick the box to share the folder and give it a share name.

If you have older clients on the network you need to keep the share name below 12 characters in length. You can then choose to allow network users to change your files. This means that they can update or even delete files. Only tick this box if you are sure you want to allow this. Figure 8-4 shows the sharing tab for a folder called Holiday 2006 that is not currently shared.

Users can see all available shared folders by going to My Network Places as shown in Figure 8-3. To access a share, just double-click on it, like any other folder.

Figure 8-3 Shares in My Network Places

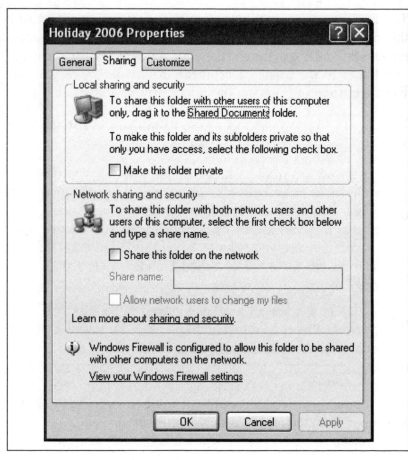

Figure 8-4 Folder sharing options tab

To stop sharing something, just follow the same steps, only this time choose either the Make this folder private option or remove the tick from the Share this folder on the network box.

Printer Sharing

Sharing a printer could not be easier. This section assumes that you have the printer already configured and connected to one of your computers. You could also have a network print server, or a wireless connection or even a Bluetooth connection to the printer. But for simplicity, let's say it is connected via a cable to the computer.

If you click Start and then Printers and Faxes, you will see any available printers that are connected and configured on the computer.

In order to share that printer with others on your network, there are two easy options.

The first is to select the printer by single-clicking it and then from the Printer Tasks menu on the left-hand side of the screen select Share this printer, as shown in Figure 8-5. The other option is to right-mouse-click the printer and select Sharing... from the menu, as shown in Figure 8-6.

Both of these options will take you to the Sharing tab of the printer properties as shown in Figure 8-7.

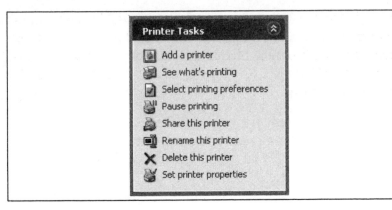

Figure 8-5 Printer tasks

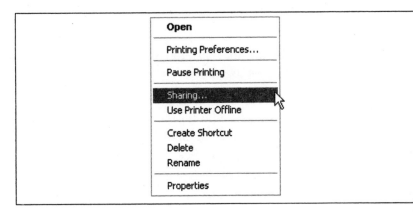

Figure 8-6 Sharing a printer

Click the Share this printer radio button and enter a suitable name for the shared printer. An example could be Laser for a laser printer or Colour if you are sharing a colour printer. If you have or are planning to have multiple printers on your network then it would be advisable to give the naming convention for them a little more thought.

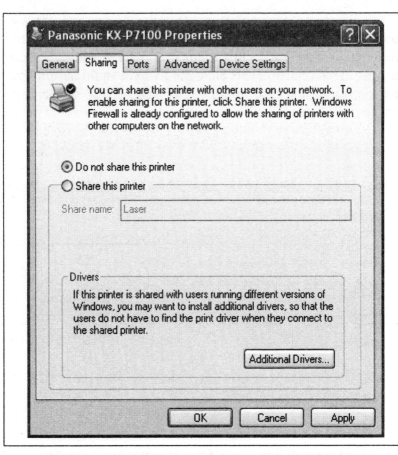

Figure 8-7 Sharing tab in printer properties

If you only have the same Windows XP client software on your network then you are done. However, if you have different versions of Windows you will need to add additional drivers. This is because when a client connects to the printer, the drivers are automatically installed on the first connection.

Figure 8-8 Additional printer drivers

To add additional drivers, click the Additional Drivers button and place a tick in the required Environment box, then click OK to complete the task as shown in Figure 8-8.

After a printer has been shared, it is shown in the Printers and Faxes area with a little hand holding the printer to denote it has been shared as shown in Figure 8-9.

Panasonic KX-P7100
0
Ready

Figure 8-9 A shared printer

To remove a share from a printer, just repeat the initial steps, only this time select the Do not share this printer radio button.

In order for the users of the other computers on your network to connect to, and use the shared printer, they must use the Add Printer Wizard and select the option for "a network printer, or a printer attached to another computer", as shown in Figure 8-10.

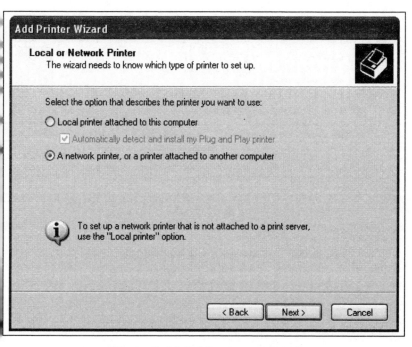

Figure 8-10 Add printer wizard

If you know the path and the share name of the printer, you can enter it on the Specify a Printer page, however, a far easier way is to just select the "Browse for a printer" option, as shown in Figure 8-11. This will then display all the shared printers that are available and allow you to select the one you want to add. This is shown in Figure 8-12.

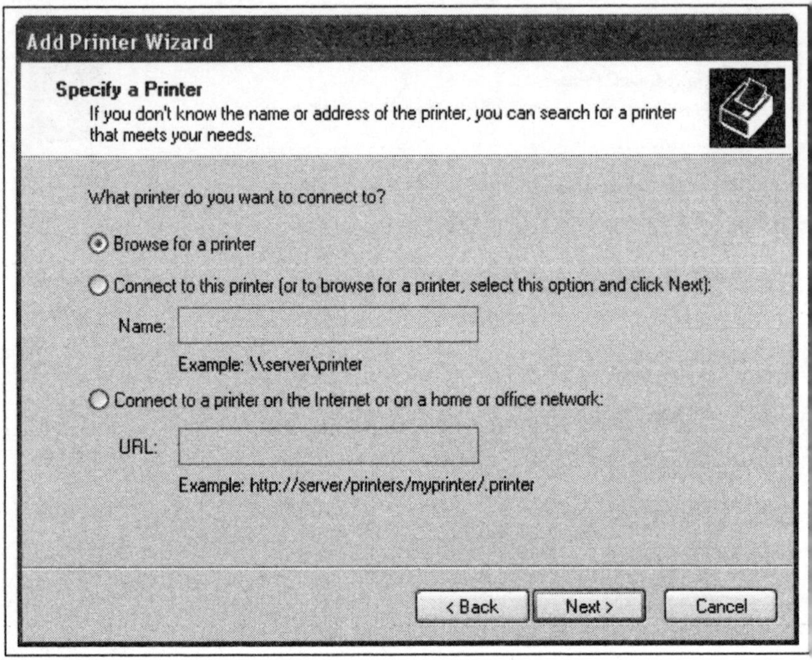

Figure 8-11 Specifying a printer

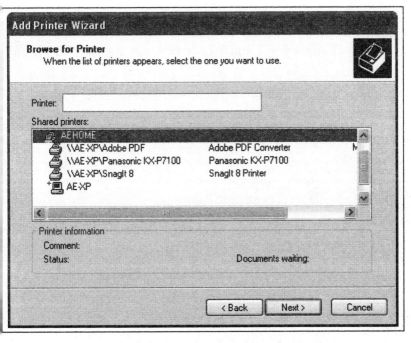

Figure 8-12 Browsing for shared printers

Email

Email is fast becoming one of those things that people use all the time and just cannot live without. For some people, it has been like that for many years.

We are not going to cover much in the way of email here as we could devote an entire book to the subject!

Instead, this brief section will explain how to quickly get started with Outlook Express, which is the built-in email client in Windows XP, and how to connect to your ISP.

You could use any other email client you want to, such as the full-blown Outlook client, or if you prefer Eudora, or any system you are comfortable with.

You will need information from your ISP for this section including account details, passwords, and the names of the POP3 and SMTP servers your ISP uses.

To start Outlook Express, click Start and select Outlook Express from the All Programs menu.

From the Tools menu, choose Accounts. This window will display any mail, news or directory service accounts you have configured, as shown in Figure 8-13.

We are going to ignore news and directory services and focus on mail.

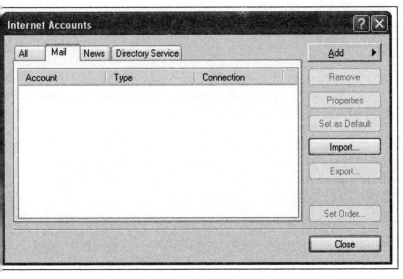

Figure 8-13 Adding a new account

Click Add and choose Mail.

You will then be asked to enter your name as you would like it displayed, as shown in Figure 8-14.

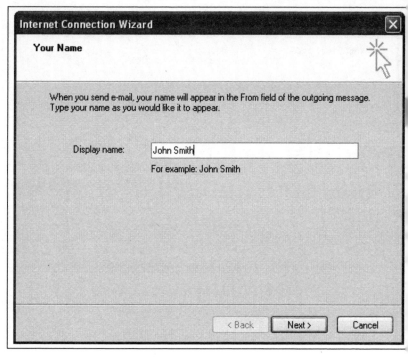

Figure 8-14 Entering your name

You will then have to enter your email address that you have been given by your ISP as shown in Figure 8-15.

Even though in Figure 8-14 and Figure 8-15 we have used John Smith as the name and someone@microsoft.com for the email address, please use your actual details. Many support calls have been logged by people entering those details instead of their own!

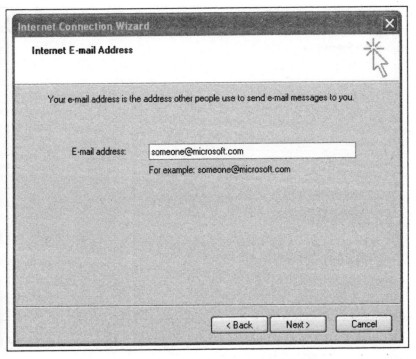

Figure 8-15 Entering your email address

Enter the Incoming mail and Outgoing mail server details on the E-mail Server Names screen as provided by your ISP, and shown in Figure 8-16.

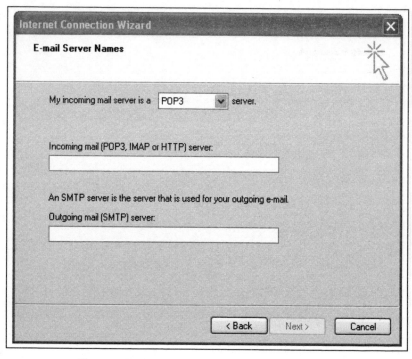

Figure 8-16 Entering e-mail server details

Finally, enter your account name and password, as supplied by your ISP, and shown in Figure 8-17. And that's it.

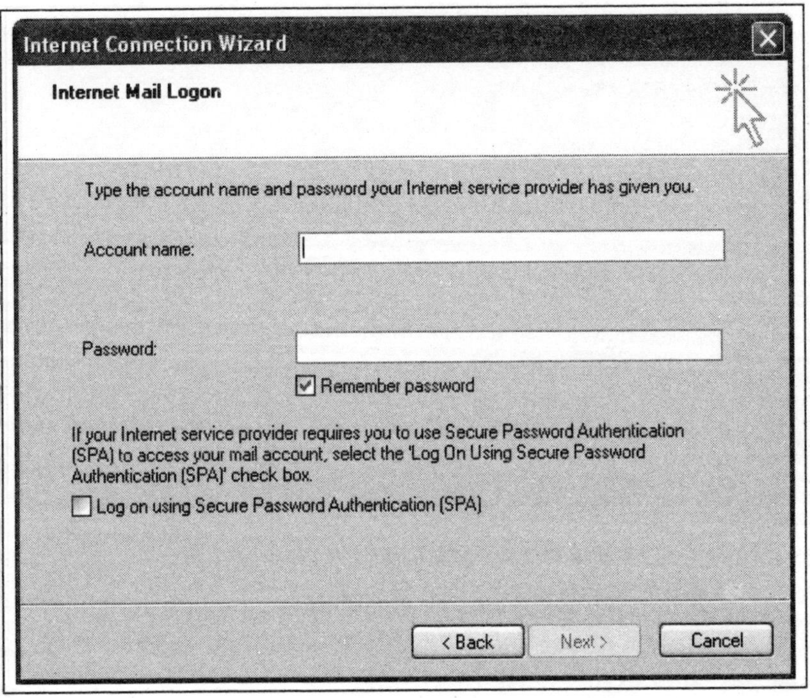

Figure 8-17 Entering account details

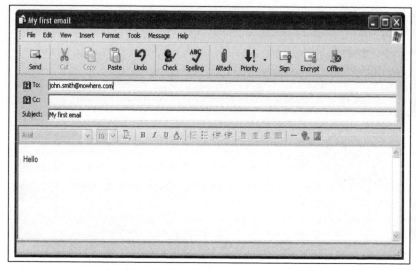

Figure 8-18 Sending your first email

All being well, and all the details having been entered correctly, you should now be able to send and receive email, as shown in Figure 8-18.

For more information on using Outlook Express, including composing emails and other additional functionality, please see the Help file within Outlook Express.

Internet Connection Sharing (ICS)

Internet Connection Sharing, or ICS, allows you to share your Internet Connection with other computers on your network, which basically means you don't have to have a direct connection for each one.

To do this, you will need two network connections. The first one will be your Local Area Network connection, and the other will be the connection to your ISP (either via a modem, a broadband router or other connection).

Figure 8-19 shows a typical ICS topology.

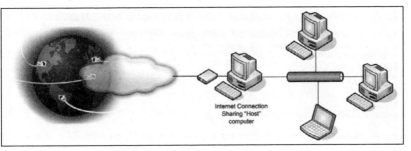

Figure 8-19 Typical ICS topology

After ICS has been configured, the computer that is acting as the ICS host will be changed to use a static IP address and all of the other computers on your network will be reconfigured to receive an IP address from this machine.

You can enable ICS in a couple of different ways. Firstly, you could click Start, Control Panel, and double-click Network Connections.

From there you can right-click the connection you want to share and choose Properties. Click on the Advanced tab and select the 'Allow other network users to connect through this computer's Internet connection' checkbox.

This is shown in Figure 8-20.

You can share a dial-up connection but it is much better to share a broadband connection, otherwise it is just too slow.

Do not use ICS if your existing network has Windows 2000 domain controllers, DNS servers or DHCP servers, or you have configured static IP addresses on your system.

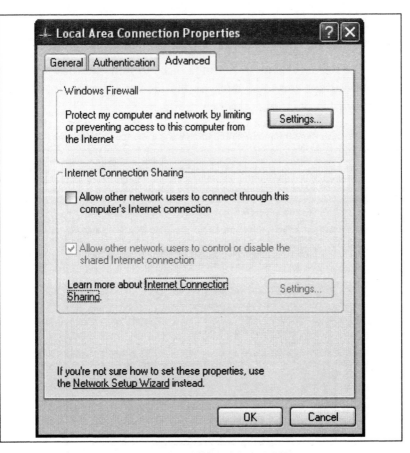

Figure 8-20 Setting up ICS

Once you have ticked the box, you can also choose whether or not to allow other network users to control or disable the shared Internet connection.

By default, this option is allowed so remember to remove the tick in the box if you don't want to allow this.

There is also a Settings box which enables you to enable certain services, such as HTTP for Internet browsing, which will be shared, as shown in Figure 8-21.

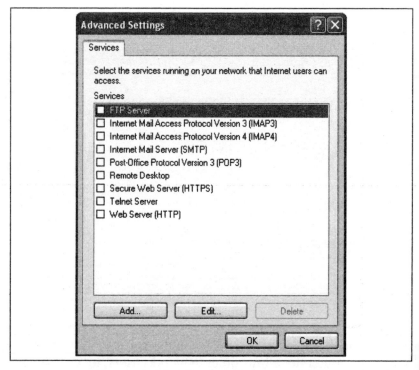

Figure 8-21 Advanced Settings of ICS

You can also add any other services yourself by clicking the Add button. This function could be very useful if you need to use a specific service, such as for an online game.

Just type in a description of the service, the name or IP address of the computer hosting this service, both the external and internal port number and also whether or not it is a TCP or UDP connection, as shown in Figure 8-22.

Figure 8-22 Adding a new service

> Don't forget, the more people that are using the
> Internet connection, the slower it may seem.

The other way, and the recommended way, is to use the
Network Setup Wizard which we have already covered in
Chapter 6.

If you want some more information on ICS, take a look
at the Help and Support section in Windows XP.

PART 6
Network Security

9

Network Security

Network security is a huge topic, and as such, this chapter is by far the largest of the whole book.

It does not matter how great or expensive your computer system is, if it is not protected properly then you could be in a heap of trouble. As the old saying goes "a chain is only as strong as its weakest link", and your network is no different.

This chapter aims to explain more about network security and how you can use software, both built-in Windows XP SP2 software, and non Microsoft software to make your system more secure.

Windows XP SP 2 Security Center

With the release of Windows XP SP 2 came a new component to XP known simply as Security Center.

Security Center specifically deals with helping you to make your XP system as secure as possible by providing a simple interface to manage Windows security settings. This interface is shown in Figure 9-1 and can be accessed by clicking Start, Control Panel and selecting Security Center.

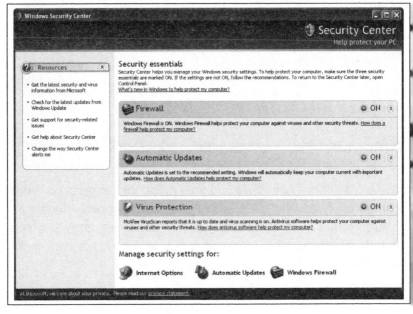

Figure 9-1 Windows Security Center

There are three core security settings, the Windows Firewall, Automatic Updates and Virus Protection. We will cover each of these in this chapter.

As you will see, if one of the settings is not enabled, it will show as OFF, however Figure 9-1 shows them all ON.

To launch any of these settings, click the required link at the bottom of the page. These links also include Internet Options which we will also cover in the this chapter.

For the Virus Protection setting, it is only for information as to what product you have installed, if any. In the case of Figure 9-1 it is McAfee VirusScan.

Other links include getting help and support from Microsoft and also accessing the Windows Update site. There is also the option to change the alert settings, as shown in Figure 9-2.

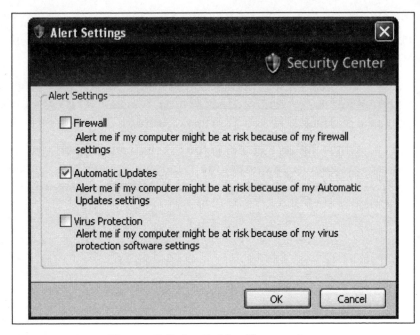

Figure 9-2 Available Alert settings

Firewalls

A Firewall is a piece of software (or hardware if you have purchased something more elaborate and expensive) that is used to prevent unauthorised access to your computer and network from any external source.

Usually, Firewalls block everything and only allow what you instruct them to allow through. These allowances are known as exceptions.

There are many software firewalls on the market now, and Windows XP even has its own built-in firewall, called, wait for it, the Windows Firewall.

The Windows Firewall that was introduced in XP SP2 is switched on by default.

If you opt to install a firewall from another manufacturer, such as Symantec, it is a good idea to switch off the Windows Firewall so that you do not have any conflicts.

You should not switch off the Windows Firewall if you do not have any other firewall running.

Even some wireless routers now come with a simple firewall installed.

The Windows Firewall

The Windows Firewall is a fairly simple to use firewall that pretty much just sits there and does what you need. When you select Windows Firewall from Security Center, you will see a page telling you the status of the firewall, as shown in Figure 9-3.

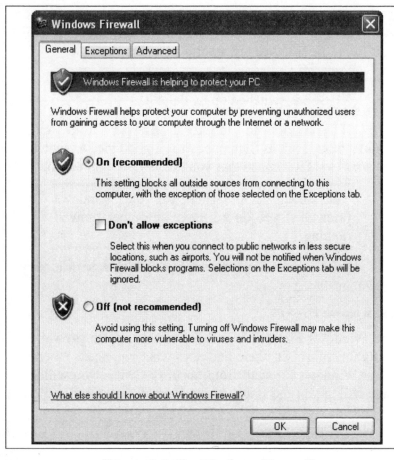

Figure 9-3 The Windows Firewall

If you click on the Exceptions tab, any exceptions that have been added either manually, or by Windows on your behalf, are displayed, as shown in Figure 9-4.

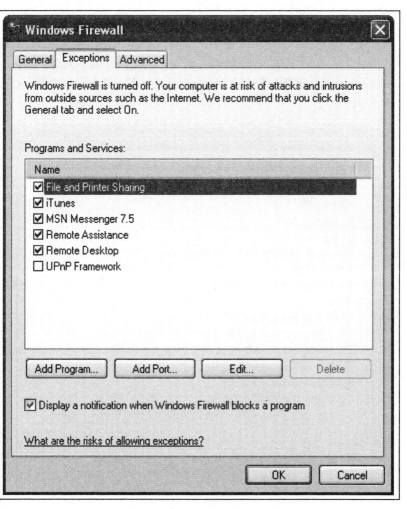

Figure 9-4 Windows Firewall exceptions

Here you can add a program or a port, edit an existing exception or even delete one.

If you click Add Program, you will be presented with a list of installed programs to choose from, as shown in Figure 9-5. If the program is not listed you can browse for it

Figure 9-5 Add a program to the exceptions

If you click Add Port, you will be presented with a dialog box, as shown in Figure 9-6. Just enter a name and the relevant port number, along with selecting if it is TCP or UDP and click OK.

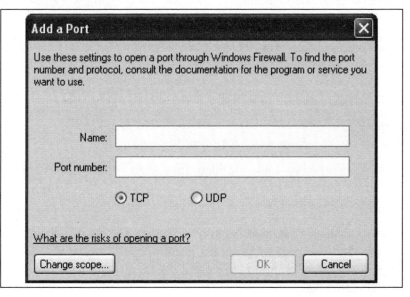

Figure 9-6 Add a port to the exceptions

If you highlight an exception and click Edit, you can choose a new path for that program, if you have moved it, as shown in Figure 9-7.

Figure 9-7 Edit a program location

You may have noticed that there is a button called Change scope on every screen. When you click this button, the change scope dialog box is displayed, as shown in Figure 9-8.

This option enables you to specify the set of computers for which the port or program is unblocked. You can choose between Any Computer, My Network or provide a Custom list of IP addresses.

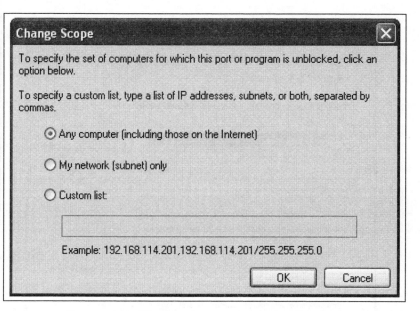

Figure 9-8 Change the scope of port blocking

The last tab in the Windows Firewall is called Advanced. This tab contains the Network Connection settings, Security Logging, ICMP and the ability to restore the firewall to its default setting. The advanced tab is shown in Figure 9-9.

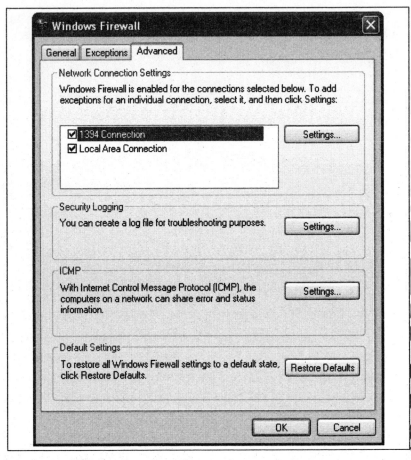

Figure 9-9 Advanced firewall configuration

The network connection settings box enables you to select which network connect the Windows Firewall is used for. A tick in the box means it is being used.

If you click settings an advanced settings dialog box is displayed showing the available services, such as Remote Desktop, Again, a tick here will indicate that it is allowed, as shown in Figure 9-10.

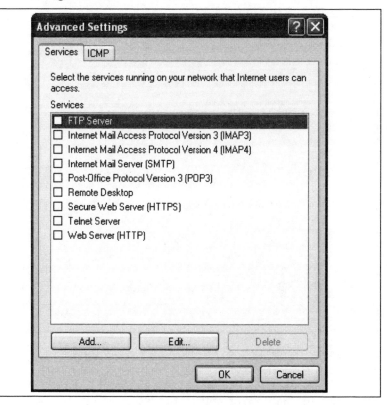

Figure 9-10 Services available through the firewall

The Security Logging settings enable you to either log dropped packets or log successful connections. By default these are turned off, so if you want to use them, remember to switch them on, and confirm the size and location of the log file, as shown in Figure 9-11.

Figure 9-11 Firewall Log settings

The ICMP settings is used to allow computers on the network to share error and status information. If you want to use this feature, just select which settings you want to allow, as shown in Figure 9-12.

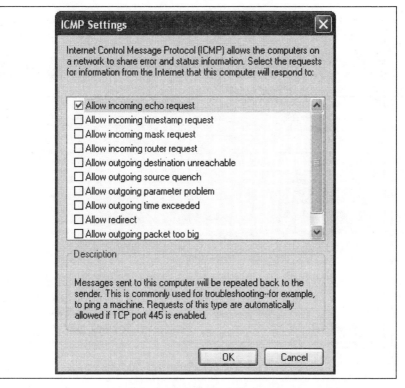

Figure 9-12 ICMP settings

Symantec Norton Personal Firewall

If for whatever reason you decide to use a firewall other than the Windows Firewall, there are lots of choices available. In order to show an example of functionality, we have chosen the Symantec Norton Personal Firewall.

Norton Personal Firewall can be purchased separately or as part of the Norton Internet Security suite of programs that also includes antivirus and antispam software, as shown in Figure 9-13.

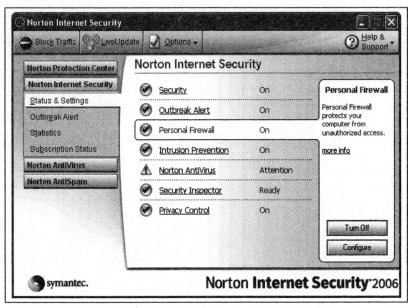

Figure 9-13 Norton Internet Security suite

Compared to the Windows Firewall, the Norton Personal Firewall has a lot more options, which for some could mean it's a lot more to configure.

As a result, one very nice feature is the learning facility, which once it's switched on, will actually learn from what you are doing and add rules automatically for you. Figure 9-14 shows the message that is displayed when a rule is created. It is worth noting however that you should examine the rules it creates just to make sure you are happy with all of them. Figure 9-15 shows the Firewall main tab.

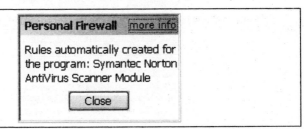

Figure 9-14 Automatic rule creation

You can also use the slider to set the firewall level. As you move the slider, information is displayed to the right which tells you about the settings. This can be very useful to help you avoid making mistakes and setting the level either too high or too low. And at any time you can click on Default Level to bring it back to how it started.

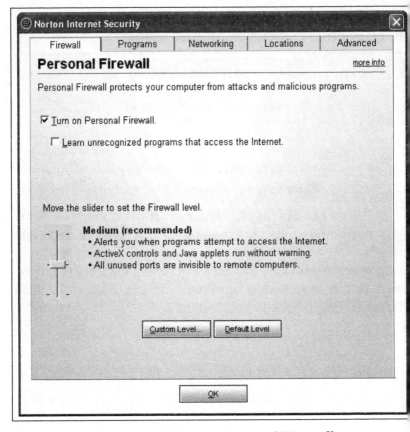

Figure 9-15 Norton Personal Firewall

Like the Windows Firewall, there is a list of programs that can use the firewall, as shown in Figure 9-16. Another nice feature is the automatic program control option which automatically allows programs to access the Internet based on a list that Symantec have identified, thus saving you a little effort.

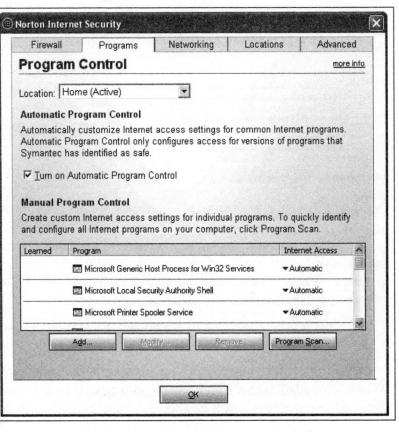

Figure 9-16 Norton Program Control

Adding a rule is very simple and a series of pages to complete are walked through for you.

We won't be going into any further detail, but suffice to say there is a lot more you can do with this, and other firewalls than can be done with the Windows Firewall, but you have to pay for it, and continue to pay for updates each year whereas the Windows Firewall is part of the operating system.

Visit http://www.symantec.com for more information on the products available from Symantec.

Automatic Updates

As anyone who has ever used Windows knows, Microsoft releases a large amount of patches for its software. These patches can include software updates, but much more importantly, and more often, they will include security patches. When new vulnerabilities are discovered in its software, Microsoft releases a patch as soon as possible.

It is a very good idea to keep your machine up to date with security patches.

In the past, you would have to visit the Microsoft Windows Update website and download whatever patches and fixes you needed. For most, this was fine. But for some, either they did not know about the site, or just did not have the time to continually check for updates.

As a result, Microsoft introduced Automatic Updates, which does exactly what it sounds like – it updates your system automatically.

Figure 9-17 shows the Automatic Updates settings.

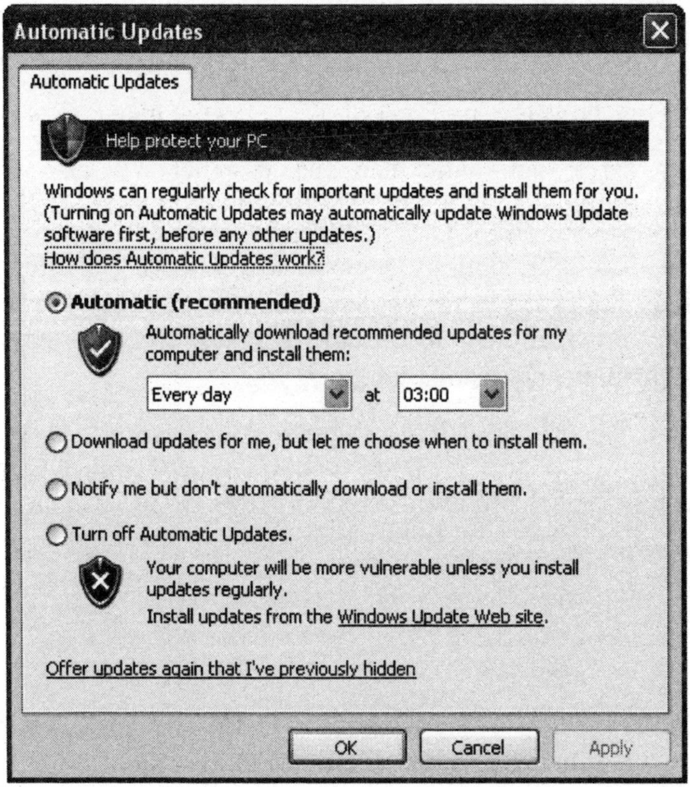

Figure 9-17 Windows Automatic Updates
options

Once you have enabled Automatic Updates, by leaving the default, and recommended setting of Automatic enabled, Windows will check the update site at 3am every day and download and install any recommended updates for you. If you don't leave your computer switched on overnight, you can of course change this to any time that is convenient, such as 9am.

Some security updates require a reboot of the system once they are installed. If you have this set to automatic then the computer will also reboot automatically.

The other options available to you are to download the updates but give you the choice when to install them, or just to notify you when new updates are available and then leave the downloading and installation up to you.

Any of these three options are preferable to having Automatic Updates switched off. If you are not sure, then select the Notify option.

It would be worth subscribing to Microsoft's Security Notification Service in order to find out about issues and vulnerabilities when they are exposed. You can subscribe by going to http://www.microsoft.com/technet/security/bull etin/notify.mspx.

Wireless Security

Naming your WLAN correctly is very important. It will be displayed within the Available Networks and is known as the Service Set Identifier (SSID). You will want to choose an SSID that is as strong as possible and not easily guessed, this helps to increase the security of your network and limit unauthorised access such as war driving.

> War driving is when a person drives around in their car with a laptop, a wireless card and an antenna and connects to someone else's wireless network.

> Make sure you change the default SSID for your wireless router as most manufacturers use the same one.

There are a couple of different ways of setting up wireless security for your network.

One way is to use the software that comes with the equipment you are using. As each will be different we won't be covering that here.

> Each wireless manufacturers' set-up and configuration could be different so it is worth checking the manual for the equipment you have before making any changes.

The other way is to use the built-in Windows network tool called the Windows XP Wireless Zero Configuration service.

Open Network Connections and right-click the Wireless Network Connection and click properties, then select the Wireless Networks tab, as shown in Figure 9-18.

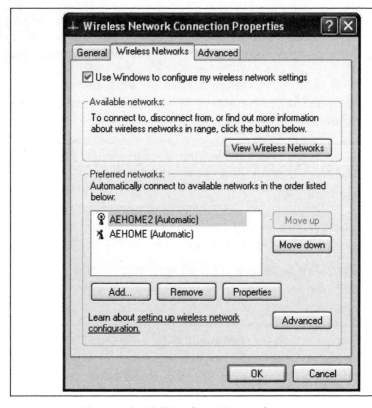

Figure 9-18 Wireless Networks properties

From here you can view all available wireless networks. Be warned however, just because you can see a WLAN, it does not mean you can connect to it. If you are doing this at home, there is a good chance that you will be able to see your neighbour's WLAN as well.

You can add a preferred network, such as your own so that your wireless computer or computers will automatically connect when they are in range. If you have more than one WLAN you can select a order of preference.

If you click on the Advanced tab, you can change what you connect to. This can be seen in Figure 9-19.

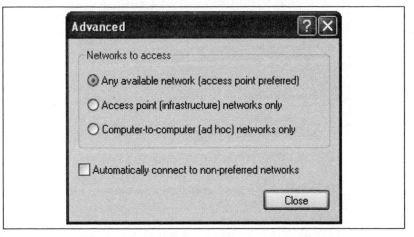

Figure 9-19 A choice of what networks to access

The one you will probably want to choose, and is also considered to be the safest option is "Access Point". This basically means that you will only be able to connect to an access point.

If you choose to look at the properties of a WLAN then you will see what is displayed in Figure 9-20.

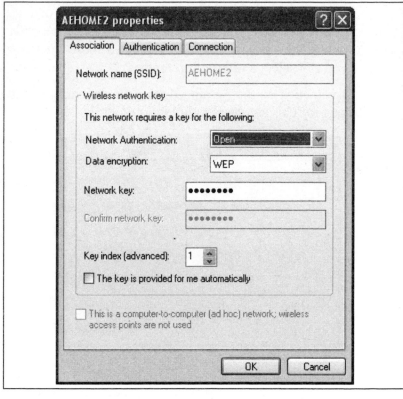

Figure 9-20 Wireless associations

This is where you choose what type of Network Authentication you are using and also what Data encryption you are using. You also enter your Network key here.

Table 9-1 shows the various options that are available.

TYPE	OPTIONS
Network Authentication	Open
	Shared
	WPA
	WPA_PSK
Data encryption	None
	WEP

Table 9-1 Wireless key options

Be aware that the more security you add to your WLAN, the more of a performance hit you receive.

Windows supports two main wireless security protocols, WEP and WMA.

WEP

WEP stands for Wired Equivalent Privacy and was designed to provide a WLAN with a level of security similar to that of a wired network. It does this by encrypting the data that is transmitted over the WLAN between the wireless client and the wireless access point.

The WEP encryption key can be 40-bit or 128-bit so check what your wireless equipment can support.

A problem with WEP is that the shared encryption key can be used in all areas of the network, and if is compromised then a hacker could gain access to the entire network. One way of reducing the risk is to change the WEP key once a month, but this means more work for you.

However, don't be put off, it is better to use WEP than nothing at all.

WPA

WPA stands for Wi-Fi Protected Access and is considered to be an improvement on WEP because it provides more sophisticated data encryption, but it also provides enhanced user authentication.

Antivirus

A virus is a piece of executable code that can cause havoc on a computer and a network. Most people remember the effects of the ILOVEYOU virus so it is imperative that you run some sort of antivirus software of all of your computers. It is not good enough to only have it running on one.

Antivirus software works by using something called a virus definition file. This file contains lists of all known virus signatures. This file is constantly updated to ensure you are always protected, so make sure you update your definition files regularly, or better yet, allow the software to do it for you.

> Windows does not yet have its own built-in antivirus product. You must buy or download a product immediately to ensure you are protected.

There are a number of antivirus products on the market, some you have to buy, and some are free to download.

Two of the biggest, and most widely used are McAfee VirusScan and Symantec Norton Antivirus.

For this section, we have used McAfee VirusScan to demonstrate what it does. It is up to you install an antivirus product before you connect to the Internet.

McAfee VirusScan

This product can be purchased separately or as part of a suite of products called Internet Security Suite.

Once you have the program installed and updated with the latest virus definition files and software updates, you can easily see how protected you are by accessing the McAfee Security Center. This give you some important information about the level of protection, including whether or not Windows Updates is enabled, as shown in Figure 9-21.

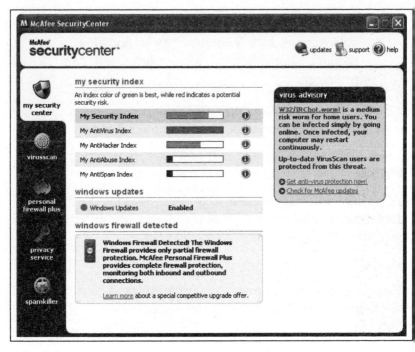

Figure 9-21 McAfee Security Center

As you can see, it also displays a message about the Windows Firewall being detected.

A green bar indicates full protection, with an amber bar showing partial protection, and red no protection at all.

If you click on the VirusScan button, you are presented with all the various options available to you, as shown in Figure 9-22.

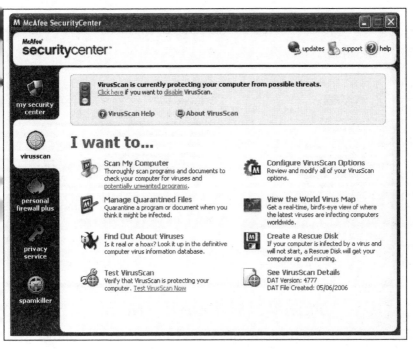

Figure 9-22 VirusScan options

If you start a scan, you have the option to select which drive or drives you want to include in the scan. You are also presented with a number of scan options, including whether or not to scan within compressed files. This is certainly worth doing because you do not want to just open a compressed file only to discover a virus within it.

Figure 9-23 shows the available scan options.

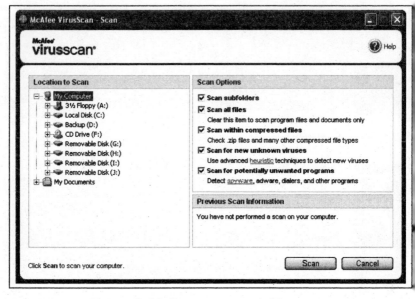

Figure 9-23 Scan options and locations

A nice feature of VirusScan is the warnings you receive if a suspicious script is detected. Sometimes people can be tricked into running some software or clicking a link which then may run a script for a nefarious purpose. This feature will inform you what the file is called and give you options, such as stopping the script or continuing what you are doing.

Figure 9-24 shows an example of this warning.

Figure 9-24 Suspicious script warning

If you click the find out more information option, you are presented with more details, as shown in Figure 9-25.

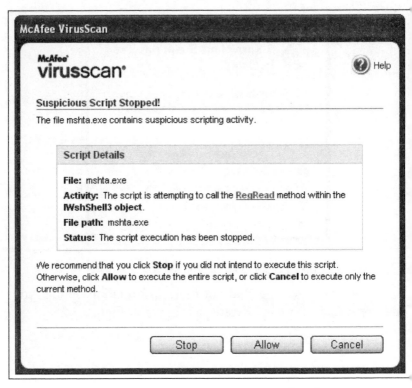

Figure 9-25 Suspicious script details

If you have any doubts at all, select Stop! In these cases it is far better to be safe than sorry.

Visit http://www.mcafee.com for more information on the products available from McAfee.

AntiSpyware

Similarly to antivirus software, it is a very good idea to run some sort of antispyware software.

Spyware is a term given to software that performs functions such as advertising, personal information collection or even changing some of your computers' settings, usually without your knowledge or consent.

Common symptoms of spyware include:

- Pop-up advertisements (also known as Adware) when you don't have a Internet browser open.

- Slow running of your computer when you are not really doing much.

- New toolbars suddenly appearing when you have not installed any new programs.

- The initial page that is displayed when you launch your Internet browser goes somewhere else and you have not changed it.

Spyware and adware is often hidden in files that you download from the Internet.

> Never download software from a source you are not sure about!

Again, there are a number of products on the market including a beta product (as of the time of writing) from Microsoft which is now called Windows Defender.

More information on Windows Defender, including downloading the beta, can be found at http://www.microsoft.com/athome/security/spyware/software/default.mspx

As with VirusScan, McAfee have a product to deal with spyware.

After you have performed a scan of a machine or drive, you are presented with a report.

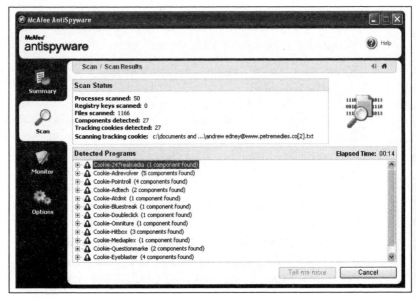

Figure 9-26 Detected spyware report

As you can see from Figure 9-26, so far 27 cookies were found on the machine. You can see more information on each one or choose to remove them.

Cookies, and how to stop them will be covered in the next section – Internet Explorer.

Internet Explorer

More than likely, unless you choose to use another browser such as Firefox, you will be using Internet Explorer to surf the Internet, order things online, download files and much more.

Internet Explorer has a number of security features that are very useful and fairly simple to use.

One of these is the ability to block pop-ups. Now most of the time pop-ups are those really annoying boxes that open new windows and tell you that you have won some amazing prize or other message to try and get you to click on it. You can now stop these messages by switching on the built-in pop-up blocker. To do this, if it is not already switched on, simply select Tools, Pop-up Blocker, Turn on Pop-up Blocker.

However, there are some legitimate uses for pop-ups, and some sites, such as Microsoft and McAfee actually use them for updating software. By default, these will also be blocked, however you can set exceptions to this rule by selecting Tools, Pop-up Blocker, Pop-up Blocker Settings, as shown in Figure 9-27.

Just enter the URL of the website, such as www.microsoft.com and click Add. You can also use wildcards (*) if you want to.

You can also select from the following filter levels:

- High : Block all pop-ups

- Medium : Block most automatic pop-ups

- Low : Allow pop-ups from Secure sites

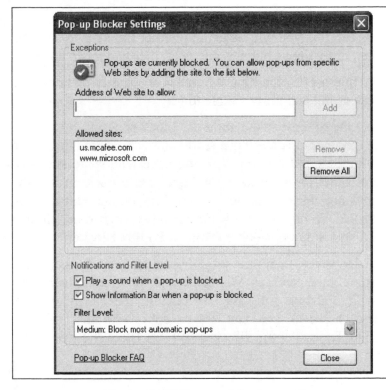

Figure 9-27 Pop-up blocker settings

You can also add sites to your exception list when you are offered the chance if Internet Explorer blocks a pop-up automatically.

Figure 9-28 shows the warning that is displayed at the top of the screen when a pop-up is blocked.

> Pop-up blocked. To see this pop-up or additional options click here...

Figure 9-28 Pop-up blocked message

If you then click this warning you have the option to temporarily allow pop-ups from the site (which will allow the pop-ups until you leave the site or close Internet Explorer) or to always allow pop-ups which adds the site details to your exceptions list.

Within Internet Explorer, there is a concept known as Zones. These zones have different settings associated with them.

To change the settings or to view the settings for each zone, select Tools, Internet Options and select the Security tab, as shown in Figure 9-29.

Then choose a zone and select Sites to view the sites with the zone, as shown in Figure 9-30 where you can also add or remove a site from the zone.

Table 9-2 shows the details of these zones.

Zone	Details
Internet	Contains all Web sites you haven't placed in other zones.
Local intranet	Contains all Web sites that are located on your organisation's intranet.
Trusted sites	Contains all Web sites that you trust not to damage your computer or data.
Restricted sites	Contains Web sites that could potentially damage your computer or data.

Table 9-2 Internet Explorer Zones

You can tell which zone you are in when viewing a website by looking at the right-hand side of the Internet Explorer status bar.

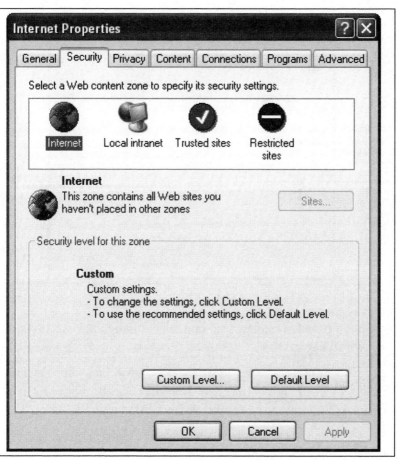

Figure 9-29 Internet Explorer Security

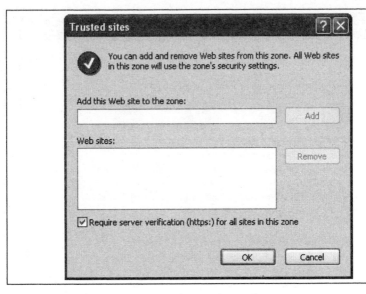

Figure 9-30 Trusted sites

For each zone, you can also change the settings, as shown in Figure 9-31.

There is a very long list of individual settings here, ranging from how Internet Explorer deals with ActiveX controls to automatic prompting for file downloads.

You can also select one of four available presets which resets the custom settings.

Remember that each zone has its own settings.

At any time you can revert back to the default settings by clicking the Default Level button.

Figure 9-31 Security settings

Every time you open a new webpage or download a file, these settings are checked.

Privacy is also a big worry when using the Internet. A lot of websites track what you access and who you are using with something called a cookie.

> A cookie is a file that can contain information such as your personal details and is stored on your computer.

You can use the slider to increase or decrease the privacy setting for the Internet zone, as shown in Figure 9-32. As you do so, an explanation is displayed so that you understand the consequences of your actions.

If you click the Sites button you can manually add a URL of a website and choose whether to block or allow cookies from that site, as shown in Figure 9-33.

If you click the Advanced button, as shown in Figure 9-34, you have the option of overriding automatic cookie handling and choosing how to deal with both first-party and third-party cookies. Unless you are really sure about what you are doing, it might be best to not change these settings and to accept automatic handling.

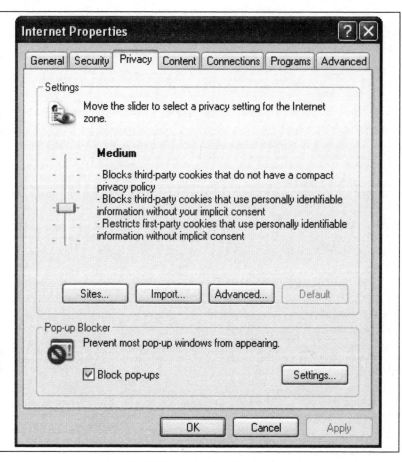

Figure 9-32 Internet Explorer Privacy

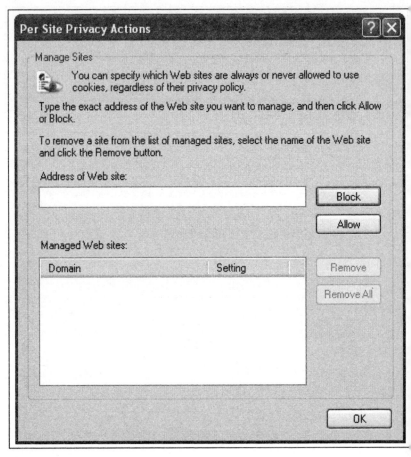

Figure 9-33 Per site privacy actions

Figure 9-34 Advanced Privacy settings

Finally, there is an Advanced tab, as shown in Figure 9-35. This tab, when you scroll all the way to the bottom has another set of security settings.

These settings include allowing active content to be run and also whether or not you want to empty the Temporary Internet Files folder when the browser is closed.

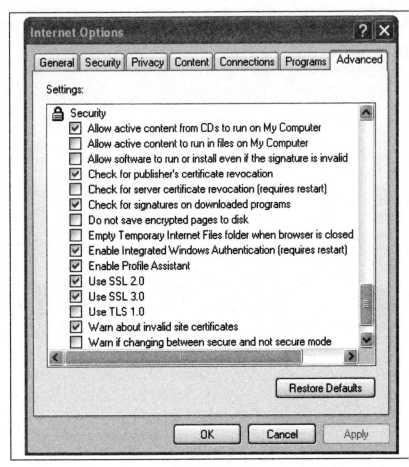

Figure 9-35 Internet Explorer Advanced settings

User Accounts

Ok, so by now you will already have at least one user account running – the one you are signed in with.

You may wish to create another account or two, or you may want to change the way the account works.

To perform these tasks and more, you use the User Accounts tool. To access it click Start, Control Panel, User Accounts and then select User Accounts, you will then be presented with the User Accounts tool, as shown in Figure 9-36.

From here you can change an existing account, create a new account and even change the way a user logs on and off.

When you are in any sub-menu of User Accounts, you can return to the main task area by clicking the Home button at the top of the page.

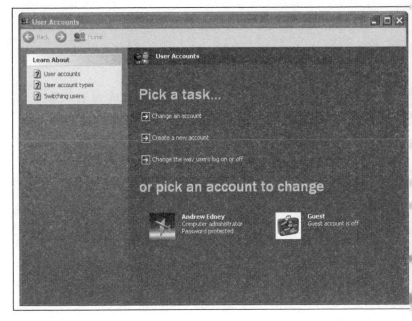

Figure 9-36 User Accounts

If you want to change something about an account, click the Change an account task and then select the account you want to change.

You will then be presented with a list of options, including the option to change the account name or type, change the password and even the picture associated with the account. All the options can be seen in Figure 9-37. All these options are fairly self explanatory so we won't go into details here.

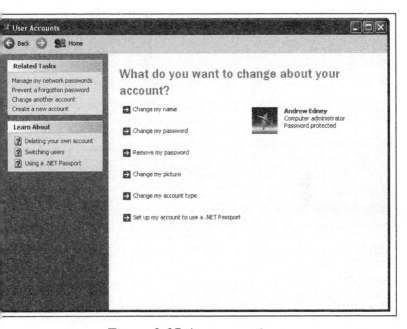

Figure 9-37 Account options

When creating or changing your password, ensure you pick a good strong password. Try not to choose something that could easily be guessed, like the name of a family member or a pet, and don't write it down and leave it near the computer.

If you want to create a new account, just click on the Create a new account from the User Accounts home page.

You will be presented with a box to enter a name for the new account. Click next to go to the account type selection screen.

Here you have the option of making the account a Computer administrator or a limited account. Table 9-3 shows the privileges granted to each of the account types.

Account Type	Privileges
Computer administrator	Create, change and delete accounts. Make system-wide changes. Install programs and access all files.
Limited	Change or remove own password. Change your picture, theme or other desktop settings. View files you created. View files in the Shared Documents folder.
Guest	Very limited access only

Table 9-3 Account types and privileges

Users with Limited accounts may not be able to install new programs.

If you are creating an account for someone else to use your computer, it may be wise to only grant them Limited status. This can be changed later if needed.

Once you have decided, just click Create Account to finish and the new account will be created and will be immediately available to use.

Should you later decide to delete that, or any other account, just click on the Delete the account option after selecting which account you want to change.

You will then have the option of keeping any files or deleting the files belonging to that account, as shown in Figure 9-38.

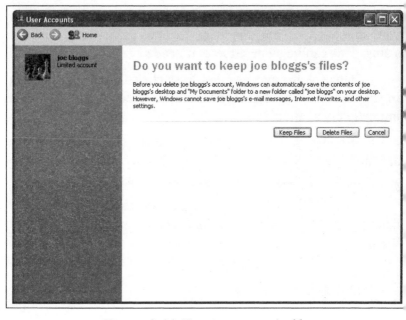

Figure 9-38 Keeping a user's files

You will then be asked to confirm that you want to perform your selected action, and then it's complete.

The other option of the home page is to change the way users logon or logoff as shown in Figure 9-39.

Here you can choose to display the Windows Welcome screen which provides a list of available users and you just have to click on whichever one you want to use and enter the password. If you turn off this feature you will have to manually enter the user name. This can certainly provide an added layer of security if you feel it's necessary in your environment.

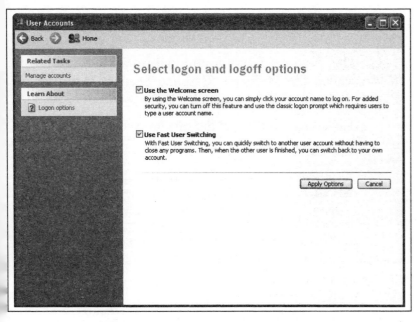

Figure 9-39 Change how users log on or off

The other option on this screen is whether or not to use Fast User Switching.

> Fast User Switching is the ability to change to another user account without having to completely logoff the system and log back on again.

System Audit with MBSA

So you have been downloading updates and installing them when you can and you have added passwords but you are not sure if you have done enough to ensure your computer is secure.

This is where a very useful tool from Microsoft comes in. It's called the Microsoft Baseline Security Analyzer, or MBSA, and best of all, it's completely free.

The current version at the time of writing is version 2.0 and can be run on Windows XP, Windows 2000 and Windows 2003.

MBSA can be downloaded from the Microsoft website: http://www.microsoft.com/mbsa

MBSA performs a number of different tasks, including scanning for common administrative vulnerabilities in not only the operating system, but also installed Microsoft software, such as Office. It also checks for security updates for those products and will advise you if you are missing any.

It also checks the strength of your passwords, what shares you have set up on your machine, and many other things including many common security misconfigurations.

For a complete list of what is scanned, have a read through the help file.

This section will walk you through running a scan and understanding its results.

After you have downloaded and installed MBSA, when you run it you will be presented with the Welcome screen, as shown in Figure 9-40.

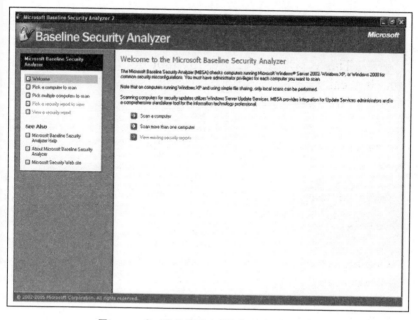

Figure 9-40 MBSA Welcome screen

From here you can choose to scan a single computer or multiple computers, and even view an existing report.

If you click on Scan a computer, you will be prompted to select the computer name you want to scan, as shown in Figure 9-41. If you click on Scan more than one computer you will see a similar screen but with Domain name instead of Computer name.

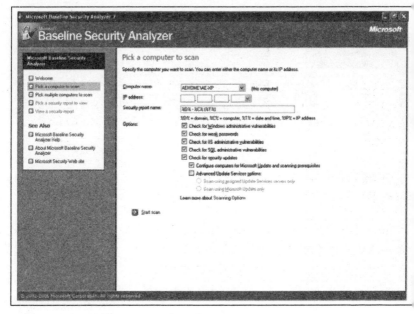

Figure 9-41 Pick a computer to scan

You can also select a number of options, such as checking for weak passwords. By default most of these settings are already enabled for you.

Table 9-4 describes these options in more detail.

Option	Details
Check for Windows administrative vulnerabilities	Scans for security issues in the Operating System, such as Guest account status, file-system type, available file shares and members of the administrator group.
Check for weak passwords	Checks for blank and weak passwords.
Check for IIS administrative vulnerabilities	Checks for security issues in IIS 5.0 and 6.0 and checks if the IIS Lockdown tool has been run.
Check for SQL administrative vulnerabilities	Checks for vulnerabilities in each instance of SQL server and MSDE.
Check for security updates	Checks for the availability of any security update.

Table 9-4 Set password options as per this table

When you are ready, just click the Start scan button to begin.

The first time you perform a scan, and periodically afterwards, security update information is downloaded from the Internet and stored on your computer.

While the scan is being performed, and be aware this can take some time, a status bar is displayed, as shown in Figure 9-42.

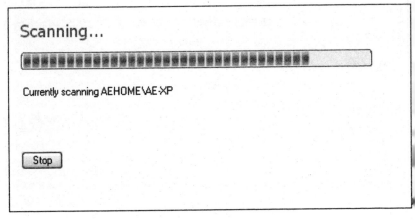

Figure 9-42 Scan status

When the scan has completed, you will be presented with a report, similar to the one in Figure 9-43.

As you scroll through the report, a green tick represents a check pass, a blue asterisk represents either a missing item or an item not approved for use in some environment, a blue "i" in a circle represents additional information, a yellow cross is a non-critical check failed and a red cross is a critical check failed. You do not want to have any red crosses!

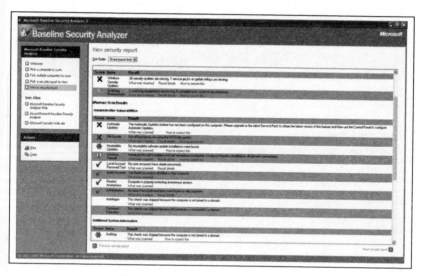

Figure 9-43 A security report

You can also choose to display the results in order from worst first! This will then give you an idea of how bad things really are. Just select 'Sort Order Score (worst first)' from the drop-down menu.

If you click on Result details on any of the items, a separate screen is displayed with additional information, as shown in Figure 9-44.

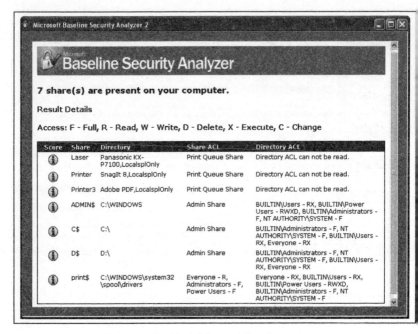

Figure 9-44 Additional information

Should you then click on any of the "i" buttons an advice screen is displayed, as shown in the example in Figure 9-45.

Shares

Issue

The Microsoft® Windows® operating systems allow users to share files with other users. However, if a share is not protected properly, unauthorized users might be able to access the information in the share.

Solution

Any shares found on the scanned computer are listed in the security report, including administrative shares. Users should review the list of shares and remove any shares that are not needed. For those shares required on the system, the share permissions should be reviewed to ensure that access is limited to authorized users only, and not shared to everyone.

Instructions

To disable a share on a computer running Windows Server 2003, Windows XP, or Windows 2000

1. Open the **Control Panel**.

2. Double-click **Administrative Tools**, and then double-click **Computer Management**.

3. Right-click the share to disable the share or change the share permissions.

Figure 9-45 More advice and guidance

All of the scan reports are stored so that you can view them again at a later time. To do this, just click on the View an existing security report button on the main page and then select the report you want to view, as shown in Figure 9-46.

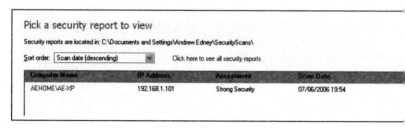

Figure 9-46 Past security reports

As you can see, an assessment is also displayed making it easy to see the status of your computer.

After you have examined the results, if you have any missing patches or updates, just pay a visit to the Windows update site at http://windowsupdate.microsoft.com or better yet, turn on automatic updates.

> It is worth running MBSA on a regular basis to ensure your computer is as secure as it could be.

Event Logs

If you have any problems with your system, be it problems with applications, security or anything else, a good place to start looking for information about the problem is in the Windows Event Logs.

The event logs record important information about your system and can be very useful when troubleshooting and diagnosing a problem.

View the event logs by clicking start, run and typing **eventvwr** which will launch the Event Viewer application or click on Start, Control Panel, Performance and Maintenance and then double-click on Administrative Tools and select Event Viewer.

The event viewer displays logs for Application, Security and System, along with any others that may have been added specifically by another program. Figure 9-47 shows the event viewer and Table 9-5 shows what is contained in each of those logs.

Log	Contains
Application	events logged by applications or programs
Security	security related events such as invalid log-on attempts
System	XP system events such as device failures

Table 9-5 Event logs

There are different types of events displayed in each log. They are Information, Warning and Error. Depending on what you are looking for, the Warning and Error messages are always a good place to start.

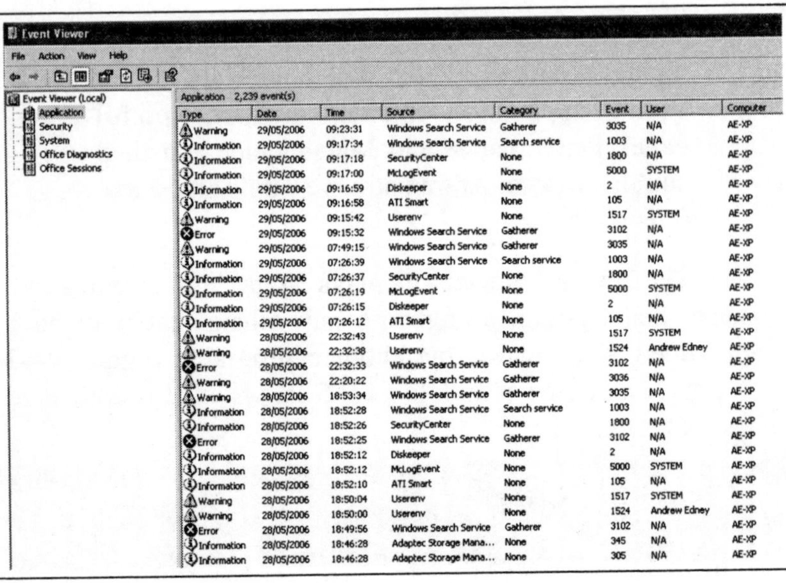

Figure 9-47 Event viewer application log

To make life easier, you can sort all the different types by just clicking on the Type tab – the same is also true for any of the other tabs.

If you want to see more information on an event, just double-click it. Figure 9-48 shows more detail on a specific event.

Sometimes the information contained in the event can be very useful – unfortunately this is not always the case and sometimes it can be of no use at all!

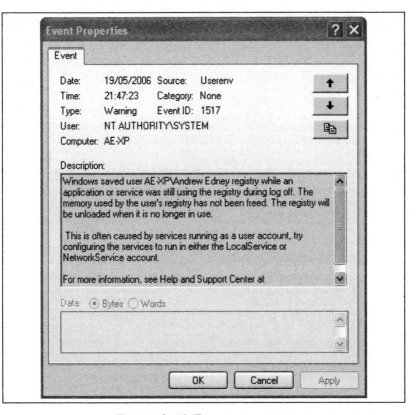

Figure 9-48 Event properties

By default, all of the logs are set to overwrite events that are older than 7 days. You can change these settings by selecting the log, such as the Security log, right-clicking and choosing properties. This will display the properties box as shown in Figure 9-49.

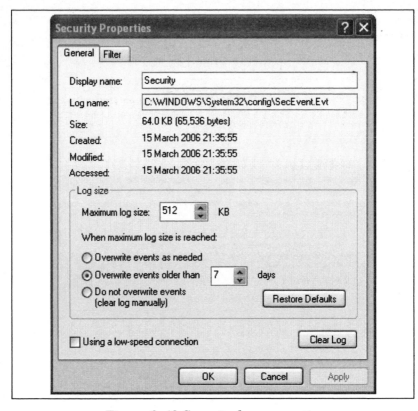

Figure 9-49 Security log properties

Here you can change the size of the log and when it is set to overwrite. You can even clear the log from here.

There is also a filter tab which enables to you filter the events so that you are not overwhelmed with everything. You may only be interested in seeing warnings and errors, and from a security standpoint, you may only be interested in seeing failures rather than successes.

Figure 9-50 shows the filter screen.

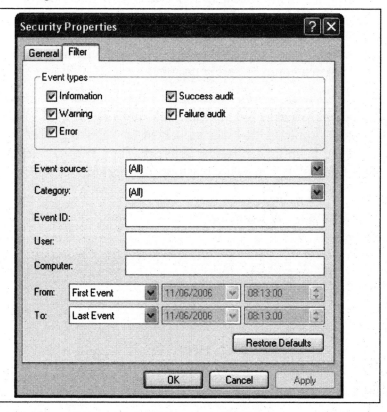

Figure 9-50 Security Log filtering

Remember that each log will have to be updated separately.

Messenger Service

One quick and easy way of making your system more secure is to switch off the Messenger Service. Now don't confuse this with the Windows Messenger Service, which provides chat capabilities. The Messenger Service is used to transmit net send and alerter service messages between clients and servers and as such could be safely disabled.

These alerter messages often appear as separate windows offering great deals and advising you of potential system problems that can be solved by "clicking here" when you are happily surfing the Internet. They are very annoying but fortunately can easily be stopped.

To do this, click Start, Control Panel, Performance and Monitoring, Administrative Tools and double-click on Services.

This displays the list of all Services and their current state, as shown in Figure 9-51.

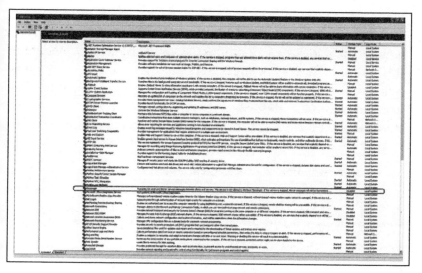

Figure 9-51 Windows Services

Scroll down through the list until you find Messenger and double-click it. This will display the properties box as shown in Figure 9-52.

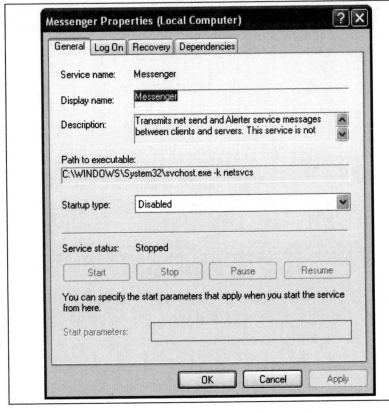

Figure 9-52 Messenger properties

All you need to do here is change the Startup type to Disabled and click OK.

> If you disable the Messenger Service you will
> no longer be able to use the Net Send command
> to send messages to other users on your
> network.

Summary

So, hopefully by now you are starting to realise just how
important security really is, assuming you did not know
already!

This is just the tip of the iceberg. You should continually be
vigilant and always ensure your software, be it operating
system or antivirus, is up to date. Run MBSA scans frequently
and have automatic updates switched on.

PART 7
Appendices and Index

Appendix A

Glossary

Term	Definition
Access Point	An access point is a device, usually wireless, that transmits and receives data.
Broadband	A high-speed communications solution used for Internet access.
Bridge	A bridge is a device that connects one local area network to another local area network that uses the same protocol.
CAT5	CAT5 is an Ethernet cable standard.
DHCP	Dynamic Host Configuration

	Protocol – a communications protocol that automatically assigns IP address to devices that support it.
Ethernet	Ethernet is the most widely used cable type in local area networks.
Hub	A hub is a device usually used to connect two or more computers together.
ISP	Internet Service Provider, for example BT or NTL.
LAN	Local Area Network – a privately owned network usually spanning the bounds of your house.
NAT	Network Address Translation – the translation of an IP address used within one network to an IP address used in another network.
NIC	Network Interface Card – the device that connects your computer to a network.
Router	A router is a device that routes data throughout a network.

Switch	A switch is a device that divides a network into different segments.
USB	Universal Serial Bus – used as a plug and play interface between a computer and an add-on device.
WAN	Wide Area Network – a privately owned network usually spanning multiple physical locations.
WEP	Wired Equivalent Privacy – a widely used wireless network security protocol.
Wi-Fi	Wireless Fidelity is a term used to describe devices that use wireless frequencies to carry their network communications.
WLAN	Wireless Local Area Network – a wireless privately owned network usually spanning the bounds of your house.
WPA	Wi-Fi Protected Access – a widely used wireless network security protocol.

Index

Hardware

Internet

Internet Explorer

Notes

Take a note of the configuration details for your equipment for future reference:

System serial number:

Windows XP serial number:

Product activation date:

Network name:

Wireless configuration details:

IP address:

Subnet mark:

Default gateway:

DNS addresses (if applicable):

Printer details:

Any other information:

Take a note of the configuration details for your equipment for future reference:

System serial number:

Windows XP serial number:

Product activation date:

Network name:

Wireless configuration details:

IP address:

Subnet mark:

Default gateway:

DNS addresses (if applicable):

Printer details:

Any other information:

Take a note of the configuration details for your equipment for future reference:

System serial number:

Windows XP serial number:

Product activation date:

Network name:

Wireless configuration details:

IP address:

Subnet mark:

Default gateway:

DNS addresses (if applicable):

Printer details:

Any other information:

Take a note of the configuration details for your equipment for future reference:

System serial number:

Windows XP serial number:

Product activation date:

Network name:

Wireless configuration details:

IP address:

Subnet mark:

Default gateway:

DNS addresses (if applicable):

Printer details:

Any other information: